THE PANIZZI LI

1992

Previously published

THE PANIZZI LECTURES
1992

Hebrew Manuscripts of East and West
Towards a Comparative Codicology
MALACHI BEIT-ARIÉ

THE BRITISH LIBRARY

First published 1993 by
The British Library
Great Russell Street
London WC1B 3DG

British Library Cataloguing in
Publication Data for this title is available.

Designed by John Mitchell
Typeset in Linotron Bembo
by Bexhill Phototypesetters, Bexhill-on-Sea
Printed in England by
Henry Ling (Printers) Ltd, Dorchester

Contents

O that record could with a backward look,
Ev'n of five hundred courses of the sun,
Show me your image in some antique book,
Since mind at first in character was done.

William Shakespeare, *Sonnets*, LIX

List of Illustrations

Colour plates

Black and white illustrations

Foreword

I prepared these lectures and the script of this small book whilst I was a Visiting Scholar at Harvard University, Cambridge (Massachusetts), enjoying the hospitality and the facilities bestowed upon me by the Center for Jewish Studies and its Director, Professor Isadore Twersky. In preparing the lectures I benefitted considerably from using the outstanding rich collections of the libraries of Harvard University, particularly Widener and Houghton Libraries.

I should like to thank the libraries which provided me with the illustrations for this publication, foremost, The British Library itself, from whose holdings originate most of the illustrations, and the following libraries: Cambridge (Mass.), Harvard College, Houghton Library; Jerusalem, Israel Museum and Heikhal Shelomo; Laon, Bibliothèque municipale; Leiden, University Library; Leipzig, Universitätsbibliothek; New York, Jewish Theological Seminary Library; Oxford, Bodleian Library and Corpus Christi College; Paris, Bibliothèque nationale; Vienna, Osterreichische Nationalbibliothek.

I wish to thank Miss Elaine M. Paintin, the Secretary of the Panizzi Foundation, for her kind and valuable assistance in coordinating my lectures and obtaining most of the illustrations.

Malachi Beit-Arié
Jerusalem 1992
The Hebrew University

Acknowledgements

The Trustees of the Panizzi Foundation would like to express their sincerest thanks to Mr J. Sterling and Mr E. Reitman for their support for the 1992 Panizzi Lectures.

The inclusion of colour plates in this publication has been made possible through the generosity of the British Friends of the Jewish National & University Library in Jerusalem on the occasion of the Library's centenary, to honour Professor Malachi Beit Arié, Director of the JNUL – 1979–1990.

PLATE 1 London, British Library MS Add. 11639, fol. 116r. King
Solomon reading a codex of the Pentateuch, Northern France, c.1280.

PLATE II Leiden, University Library MS Or. 4725, fol. 1r. Bilingual Psalter: Latin, Hebrew and abridged *Breviarum in Psalmos*, England, mid-twelfth century.

PLATE III Paris, Bibliothèque nationale hébr. 1196, fol. 5v. Decorated
initial letters in Latin characters, Provence, 1420.

xiii

Medieval Hebrew Manuscripts as Cross-Cultural Agents

I SHOULD like to thank the Panizzi Foundation and its Selecting Committee for inviting me to deliver the Panizzi Lectures this year. This is not merely gratitude for the honour conferred on me personally, but more particularly for the privilege and the opportunity to represent the cultural heritage of a minority and describe some facets of its diversified and not very well known manifestations.

Hebrew handwritten books are medieval artifacts, 'sheathes of wisdom', according to a metaphor of the Spanish Hebrew poet Moses Ibn Ezra (c.1055–after 1135), produced by a religious, ethnic and cultural minority – the Jewish people. Like all other medieval books they display technical practices, calligraphic and artistic skills and mirror the intellectual activity and interests of the marginal Jewish society of their time and region of production. Yet, extraordinary historical circumstances dispersed the Jewish communities around the Mediterranean basin and further eastward, northward and westward, interweaving them within various civilizations, religions, and cultures, and transplanting them within others.

Flourishing or impoverished, secure or oppressed and harassed, small and large Jewish communities were spread out during the Middle Ages from central Asia in the east to England in the west, from Yemen and North Africa in the south to Germany and central and Eastern Europe (in the late Middle Ages) in the north, embraced by the great civilizations of Islam and Christianity, the Latin West, the Byzantine East, and many other minor cultures, languages and scripts. Notwithstanding their firm adherence to their unique religion, language, culture and customs, their self-government and educational system, they were strongly influenced by the surrounding societies and shared with them not only goods, tools, crafts and techniques, but also literary styles, aesthetic values, philosophical theories and principles and calligraphic fashions. The mobility of individual Jews, by choice or by economic necessity, and of entire communities, by force, made them agents of cross-cultural contacts and influences and intercultural confrontations.

The Jews have always remained loyal to their own script, despite the adoption of the spoken languages of their accommodating societies in everyday life, the integration of the Western and Eastern dialects of the Aramaic language in their post-biblical literature; the wide use of Greek by Hellenized Jews in late antiquity; the extensive employment of Arabic as the main written language in countries under Muslim rule; and later, to a much lesser extent, the application of European vernacular languages – the Romance languages and German – in their literature. Ever since their old script, derived from the Phoenician, was replaced in the late third century BC by an offshoot of the Aramaic script,[1] the Jews have adhered to this Semitic national writing rendering in it not only literary texts and documents written in the Hebrew language, but also other borrowed languages, including the European ones, in transcription.

To be sure, Jews in late antiquity in the East and until the ninth century in the West did employ other scripts, particularly Greek, for their non-book records. This is attested by many documents and inscriptions, mostly funerary, found in Palestine and Egypt, and hundreds of inscriptions preserved mainly in Rome, but also in other areas in the Orient, like Syria and south Arabia, Asia Minor, the Greek islands and the Balkans, Italy, Sicily, Sardinia, Malta, Spain, France and even Germany.[2] In

Hellenistic, Roman and Byzantine Palestine the Jews sometimes used other Semitic scripts and languages for inscriptions and documents, and extensively Greek, but wrote their literary texts exclusively in the Hebrew language and script, as the Dead Sea Library clearly demonstrates. Both in Sassanian Babylonia and Roman and Byzantine Palestine they composed their post-biblical legal, exegetical and Midrashic literature in Hebrew dominated by adopted Aramaic dialects written in Hebrew characters. The Greek language and script were widely used in documents in Egypt, where Hellenized Jews like Philo of Alexandria composed their literary works in Greek, and also in funerary inscriptions found elsewhere in the East and the West, which reflect the Hellenization of the Jewish communities in all the areas around the Mediterranean. In the inscriptions surviving outside Palestine and its vicinities, Hebrew was rarely employed in late antiquity and the early Middle Ages, and its use was usually limited to short formulae, while Latin was used considerably in Italy, and elsewhere in Europe, as is attested, for instance, by the rare burial inscriptions found in France.[3]

However, surviving epigraphic records show that at the beginning of the Middle Ages Hebrew gradually replaced Greek and Latin in Christian countries, and since the central Middle Ages European Jews have used the Hebrew script exclusively for their epigraphic writings, as for literary texts and documents. Charters and deeds of financial and property transactions between Jews and Gentiles, particularly quitclaims, preserved in England from the late twelfth century until the expulsion of the Jews in 1290,[4] and in Christian Spain, mainly Catalonia, from the eleventh century,[5] not only demonstrate the adherence of the Jews to their script and language, but reflect their lack of knowledge of Latin. These records are always bilingual and bi-scriptual. The detailed document is written in Latin (or, occasionally, in England, in Norman-French), accompanied sometimes by a duplicate record, but usually by a shorter version, or just an endorsement, or even only a signature, in Hebrew (*see* Figs. 1 and 2).

In the countries of the Latin West some learned Jews must have been proficient in Latin in the late Middle Ages, as is

Fig. 1 London, British Library MS Harley Chart. 43A, 60A and B. Latin charter and its accompanying Hebrew quitclaim of debt, Lincolnshire, 1232.

Fig. 2 London, British Library MS Harley Chart. 77D, 40. Hebrew quitclaim of land attached by a seal to a Latin charter, England, 1239.

testified by the Hebrew translations of Latin works of philosophy, theology, mathematics, astronomy and medicine, made mostly in Spain, Provence and Italy, as well as by the influence of Western philosophy, Christian mysticism and various literary trends which can be discerned in Hebrew literature. Moreover, in southern Italy Jewish translators and philosophers were employed by Frederick II in Sicily. They were associated with the scholarly initiatives of the Angevin kings, Charles I and Robert of Anjou in Naples, and translated Arabic texts into Latin for them.[6] However, learned Jews in medieval Christian Europe apparently never employed the Latin script, nor did they use the Latin language in Hebrew transcription. On the other hand, from the eleventh century onwards Jews did employ occasionally, and in the late Middle Ages more extensively, the vernacular languages of their environments, transcribing them in Hebrew characters.

Old French, Provençal, Catalan, Castilian, Spanish and Italian, Greek and particularly Old High German were assimilated by the Jews, 'Judaized' and incorporated into their Hebrew written texts. At first they were used in exegetical, lexigraphical and halakhic works, which were interspersed with vernacular words primarily to specify an object, and in biblical glossaries and glossed bibles. Then the vernacular languages were

5

exploited to cater to the needs of the masses and the less educated strata and provide them with complete translations of Hebrew biblical books, daily prayers, ethical, grammatical and medical treatises, and, later, even with popular literature originally composed in the vernaculars, but always rendered in Hebrew transcription. The earliest use of vernacular languages goes back to the eleventh century, a period from which very few Romance texts are extant, and thus serves as a most valuable source for the history of those languages.[7]

Things were different in the vast territories dominated by Islam. The remarkable diffusion of Arabic in the Middle East, North Africa and Spain did not bypass the Jews, who soon adopted Arabic in daily communication. Jewish scholars acquired a knowledge of Arabic literature, which became a storehouse for much of the world's knowledge and learning through translations of Greek, Syriac, Pahlavi and Hindi works. Learned Jews acquired the Arabic script and sometimes used it for commercial records and letters,[8] owned books by Muslim writers in Arabic, and in Spain occasionally even copied them,[9] but would usually transliterate them in Hebrew characters, as they did while writing their own Hebrew literary texts. Moreover, they adopted Arabic as their main scholarly language, employing it in many important works of biblical and talmudic commentaries, Jewish law, philosophy, lexicography and sciences written in the countries under Muslim rule.[10] Yet, except for some early Jewish philosophers and scientists who published medical and astronomical works destined for the non-Jewish public in Arabic script, all those Judeo-Arabic works were written and disseminated in the Hebrew script.[11]

An exception were some of the Arabic works written by the Karaites, a rejected Jewish sect which came into being in the eighth century, denying talmudic tradition and teachings and adhering to the Hebrew Bible as the sole source of Jewish creed and law. Karaite Hebrew works were written in Hebrew script, and so were many of their Arabic works and documents. However, motivated by their hostility to the Rabbinical institutions and their quest for a distinct sectarian identity, certain circles in the tenth and eleventh centuries regularly wrote

Karaite Arabic works in Arabic script. Though they sometimes rendered Hebrew quotations in Hebrew characters, they even wrote biblical and liturgical Hebrew texts entirely in Arabic transcription.[12]

Thus, in the Middle Ages the Jews everywhere, in East and West, utilized the Hebrew script, from the ninth century rather exclusively, for written communication, documentation, legal proceedings and particularly for writing their literature and disseminating it, mainly in Hebrew, but also in other languages, especially Arabic. This remarkable phenomenon, together with the vast territorial dispersion of the Jews, turned a minor[13] marginal script and booklore into a geographically rather major one. From the viewpoint of extent and diffusion the Hebrew script was employed in the Middle Ages over a larger territorial range than the Greek, Latin or Arabic scripts, as Hebrew manuscripts and documents were produced within and across all these and other script zones.

The paradoxically humble and obscure 'empire' of this marginal Hebrew script and booklore naturally encompassed diversified regional shapes, types and styles of the common script, the handwritten book and the scribal practices involved in its production. Medieval Hebrew books shared the same script, but were divided by different geo-cultural traditions of production, design and writing modes, strongly influenced by contacts with local dominating non-Jewish values and practices. Hebrew manuscripts indeed present a solid diversity of well differentiated script types,[14] technical practices,[15] and scribal designs, moulded by the different places where they were made. Moreover, they also bear witness to the mobility of Jewish scribes and copyists, who crossed political frontiers and cultural borders, carrying with them their native scripts and scribal practices, cultural heritage and artistic influences, and introducing them into other areas. Systematic study of almost all the extant dated medieval Hebrew manuscripts[16] has revealed that about one-fifth of them were written by immigrant scribes, who retained their native type of script,[17] graphic habits and scribal formulas, while inevitably adopting local codicological practices such as writing materials, format, quiring and ruling techniques.[18] In certain areas and periods the percentage of immigrant scribes was much higher, as in fifteenth-century Italy, where the manuscripts produced by scribes originating from Spain, Provence, northern France and Germany constitute nearly half the extant dated manuscripts.

A striking illustration of these intricate circumstances of the employment of the Hebrew script and Jewish cross-cultural mobility is to be found in MS Oxford, Corpus Christi College 133, a copy of a Hebrew prayer-book, produced in the twelfth century, or earlier, perhaps in Germany. On two pages which were left blank (fols. 350r and 249v), a Jewish creditor living in England recorded payments made to him at the end of the twelfth century by various Englishmen, including three bishops, in areas extending from Bath to Norwich and from Exeter to Winchester. What is striking is that the records were written by the owner of this prayer-book of apparently German rite in Arabic, rendered in Hebrew characters, in a cursive Spanish-Andalusian type of script![19] This manuscript, which mirrors the vicissitudes of unstable Jewish existence and demonstrates the complexity of Hebrew palaeography, may very well be found to contain the only document in Arabic in medieval England.

About 70,000 handwritten Hebrew books, part of them incomplete and fragmentary, but many including several different copies bound together, have survived to this day. They are kept in some six hundred national, state, public, municipal, university and monastic libraries and private collections all over the world. England can boast of having some of the finest and most important treasures of Hebrew manuscripts, mostly concentrated in 'the golden triangle' of The British Library, London, the Bodleian Library, Oxford, and Cambridge University Library.[20] Not all those manuscripts are medieval. Many, perhaps up to half of them, are post-medieval, and part of them are late handwritten books, usually copies of unprinted texts. In addition, some 150,000 medieval literary fragments were preserved in the Cairo Geniza, in a store room for worn-out books in the Ben Ezra synagogue of the Palestinian community in Fustat (old Cairo) and also partly in the Jewish cemetery there. The majority of these are kept in Cambridge University Library. In recent years numerous remains of medieval European Hebrew books are being recovered in Italian archives, where sheets removed from disbound confiscated manuscripts were used as register bindings (*see* Fig. 3).[21] Similarly, many other parchment fragments can be found in Latin manuscripts and printed books in various European collections, in which they served as fly-leaves, binding, or were pasted to the inner covers.

This quantity of surviving Hebrew medieval books represents of course a very small portion of the entire book production of the Jewish people, which, due to its communal system of education, was generally literate.[22] The loss of most of the handwritten codices was not the consequence of historical conditions alone. Hebrew books were not only destroyed or abandoned through wanderings, emigration, persecution, pogroms and expulsions, or confiscated and set on fire in Christian countries, particularly France and Italy,[23] but were foremost worn out by use. Unlike Latin, Greek and, to a certain degree, Arabic books, they were preserved neither in royal or aristocratic collections, nor in monasteries, mosques, religious or academic institutions, but were privately owned for practical use, consultation and study. The discovery of the Cairo Geniza provided us with a tangible sample of the extent of book consumption among medieval Jews. The bulk of the fragments was stored over a period of about 250 years, between 1000 and 1250,[24] and constitutes the remains of some 30,000–40,000 books which were used, worn out and buried by one sector of one Jewish community – important as it was – in one city alone.

Furthermore, the number of extant medieval codices and fragments, which adds up to over 100,000 copies, represents Hebrew book production of the last six centuries of the Middle Ages only. The revolutionary book form of the codex, which had already been promoted and spread by Christians in the first centuries of our era and had replaced the old form of the roll in areas around the Mediterranean from about 300,[25] was adopted by the Jews much later, as is shown both by findings and by

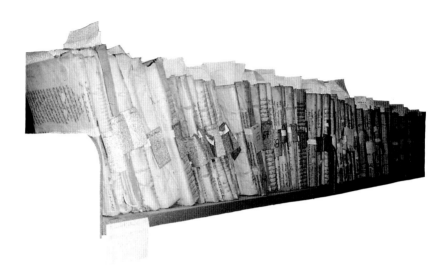

Fig. 3 Italian registers covered by parchment leaves taken from Hebrew manuscripts. Bologna, Archivo di Stato. Courtesy of Prof. M. Perani.

literary and textual evidence. Between the rich finds of Hebrew books from late antiquity, namely the Dead Sea Scrolls and fragments from the Qumran caves and the Judean Desert of the Hellenistic and early Roman period, and the earliest dated and datable surviving Hebrew codices, there is a salient gap of some eight hundred years almost without extant witnesses of the Hebrew book. Not even one of the few dozen existing literary fragments, dating from this lacuna, mainly papyri of the Byzantine period excavated in Egypt, derives from a codex.[26]

All references to books in the rich talmudic literature, both of Palestine and Babylonia, relate to scrolls, and only a few isolated passages use metaphorically the Greek term of *pinax,* apparently meant to designate a concertina-like multi-plate writing device, more like a scroll than a codex.[27] Other scarce talmudic sources probably refer to documentary and perhaps also liturgical rolls which unfold vertically, described as written 'transversa charta' in Latin sources, and, following Lloyd Daly and Sir Eric Turner, are termed *rotuli*. The use of such rolls, as pharaonic, Ptolemaic, Hellenistic and Roman papyri show, was confined to documentary functions in antiquity and to a great extent in the early Middle Ages.[28] But, like the adoption of the *rotulus* format for Christian Byzantine liturgy in Greek and Latin from the ninth century,[29] and its partial use by Muslims in the Orient as early as the eighth century for copies of parts of the Koran and literary texts,[30] dozens of early Geniza literary and liturgical parchment fragments (and some later ones on paper) originate from *rotulus* books,[31] and may imply that this book format was employed by the Jews in the late transition period between the scroll and the codex.

In fact, the earliest reference to the codex form in Jewish literature does not date before the end of the eighth or the beginning of the ninth century. Moreover, the earliest term designating a codex was borrowed from Arabic and persisted in the Orient for quite a long time.[32] Therefore it seems that the Jews in the East adopted the codex after the Arabic conquest, very likely not before the ninth century or a little earlier.

This late adoption of the much more convenient, capacious, durable, easy to store, carry about, open and refer to book form can be explained by assuming that the Jews adhered to the rollbook in order to differ from the Christians, who first used the codex for disseminating the New Testament and the trans-lated Old Testament. Indeed, the *Sefer Tora,* the Pentateuch used for liturgical readings in synagogues, and some other biblical books, are written to this day on scrolls. But the late employ-ment of the codex may very well reflect the basically oral nature of the transmission of Hebrew post-biblical, talmudic and midrashic literature, which is explicitly testified by some sources, and implied by the literary structures and patterns, mnemonic devices and diversified versions of this literature.

Indeed, the earliest extant, explicitly dated Hebrew codices were written at the beginning of the tenth century,[33] all of them in the Middle East. From the eleventh century onwards dated manuscripts have survived from Italy and the Maghreb, while those produced in the Iberian peninsula, France, Germany,

England and Byzantium date from the twelfth century onwards. Until the thirteenth century their number is rather small, particularly outside the Middle East, but it grows, thereafter, reaching a peak in the fifteenth century, during which about half the dated codices produced until 1540 originated.[34] Thus, the history of the medieval Hebrew book and Hebrew medieval palaeography is inescapably confined to the late Middle Ages. The dated manuscripts, which comprise about one tenth of the extant medieval books, and the undated ones, which can be located and approximately dated through the typology drawn from the dated manuscripts, furnish us with solid knowledge of the crystallized types of book scripts, scribal practices and codicological techniques of the late Middle Ages. Though we do have significant information on the earlier stages of book production and script in the Orient, we lack such knowledge concerning the formative period elsewhere.

In compensation for this drawback of Hebrew medieval palaeography and codicology, the manuscripts supply us with much more precise and first-hand information regarding book production than do Latin manuscripts. The proportion of explicitly dated copies is much higher among Hebrew manuscripts. Their scribes provide far more information in their colophons, usually indicating their name and the names of those who commissioned the copying, specifying the locality where the copy was made in about half of the dated manuscripts, and occasionally letting us know their fees, copying speed, the quality of their models and their critical ways of reproducing the text.

Above all, Hebrew medieval handwritten books reflect not only the multi-faceted, marginal Jewish culture, but also scribal traditions, technical practices, principles of book design and calligraphic fashions of the major and some minor civilizations and cultures in the East and the West. They bear witness to medieval cross-cultural contacts, influences and inspiration, and to a shared heritage, not only by their technique, design, aesthetic values, calligraphic style, decoration and illumination, but also by their contents and languages. They disseminated many Latin, Greek and Arabic philosophical and scientific works and even the popular literature of various countries in Hebrew translations,[35] as well as Arabic, Persian and European vernacular texts transcribed in Hebrew script. Bridging between East and West, between Islam and Christianity, between Arabic, Latin, Greek, as well as Coptic, Syriac, Persian, Armenian and Slavic booklore, Hebrew manuscripts may very well prove a useful tool for intercultural study and comparative palaeography and codicology.

In the following lectures I shall present before you the various types and modes of medieval Hebrew book script and some designs and codicological features of Hebrew manuscripts, comparing them to Latin, Arabic and Greek writings, book design and techniques and indeed pointing out their noticeable influences. However, one should not entirely rule out the possibility that contemporarily shared or similar writing styles and technical practices of book production in different cultures of the same area do not necessarily mean intercultural scribal borrowing, but might have been independent outcomes of common aesthetic and technical impulses of the *Zeitgeist*. Were there actually contacts between Jewish and non-Jewish scribes during the Middle Ages?

In the Muslim territories, where Jews used the Arabic language extensively and occasionally its script, and owned, commissioned and even sometimes copied Arabic manuscripts, direct scribal contacts were most likely inevitable, though we do not seem to have explicit evidence of scribal association between Jews and Muslims. Paradoxically, in the Christian countries, where Jews never used the Latin script, copied or owned Latin manuscripts, except as pawns, and were socially secluded and often persecuted, we do have some tangible evidence of immediate contacts between Hebrew and Latin scribes and book artists. These striking testimonies demonstrate more than merely scribal contacts. In fact, they reflect scribal association and cooperation which might modify the common image of the cultural ties between Jews and Christians in the

Middle Ages, and I should like to introduce some of those testimonies before concluding my introduction. I shall start with the earliest example, dating back to the Carolingian period.

As I have implied, no dated or datable finds of Hebrew books or documentary scripts clearly originating in the zone of the Latin West have survived from periods before the late eleventh century. However, by sheer luck I have come across a very short, but most rewarding, record of Hebrew writing from ninth-century France in an unexpected source. MS 407 of the Municipal Library of Laon (France) is a Latin manuscript which contains copies of episcopal epistles, mainly written by Hincmar, the Bishop of Rheims (c.806–882), Charles the Bald's most important political adviser, or sent to him by Popes, archbishops and synods, as well as correspondence between Charles the Great and Charles the Bald and their contemporary Popes.[36] On the upper margin of one written page (*see* Fig.4) and on another page left blank in the manuscript, ten Hebrew words, comprising the beginning of a biblical verse, a post-biblical word and a conflation of two other memorized biblical verses, were neatly written by a qualified, undoubtedly Jewish, hand.[37] The manuscript, written by a professional scribe, was Hincmar's own copy, or a copy authorized by him, as is evident from some marginal notes in his own hand. However, like many other ninth-century manuscripts in the Laon Municipal Library, it had most probably belonged to the library of Charles the Bald, and after his death in 877 was donated to the cathedral of Laon, the capital of the Carolingian kings since the time of Charles the Bald, where it was kept until the French revolution[38]. Therefore, it is most unlikely that such a prestigious royal and clerical book would have ever been possessed by a Jew, even a pawnbroker. The only possible circumstances which could have enabled a Jew to neatly jot Hebrew writing in such a highly official copy must have involved the intimate association of a Jewish scribe, or, more likely, a scholar, either with Hincmar's scribal circle, or more probably, with Charles the Bald's library or court. This modest record, which gives us our only example, poor as it is, of 'Carolingian' Hebrew writing, may also provide additional evidence of Jews employed by Charles the Bald.[39]

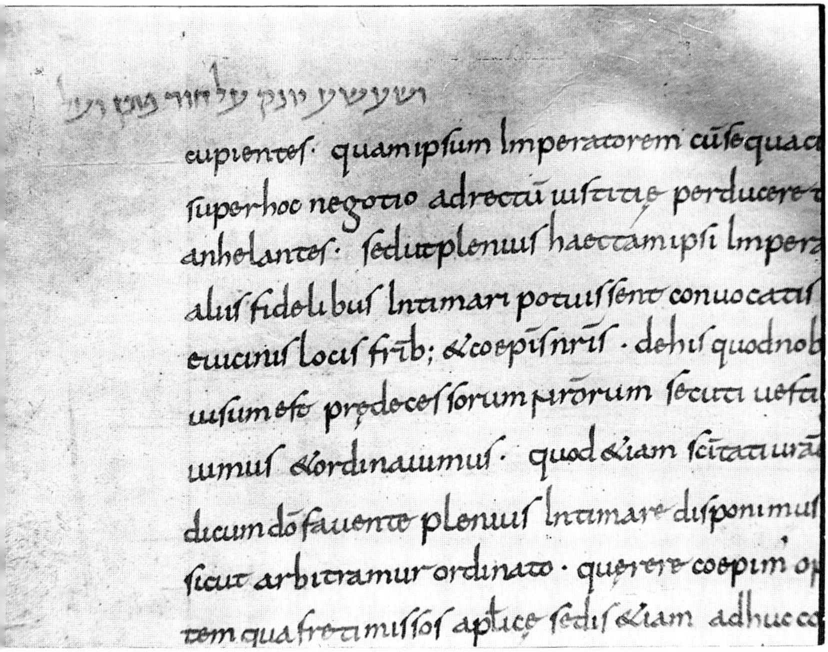

cupientef· quamipfum Imperatorem cūfequa
fuperhoc negotio adrectū uifcitif perducere
anhelantef· fedutplenuif haectamipfi Imper
aluffidelibuf Intimari potuiffent conuocatif
eucunuf locuf frb; &coepifnrif· dehif quodnob
ufum efe prędecefforum prorum fecuti uefa
uimuf &ordinauimuf· quod &iam fcitatiurā
dicumdōfauente plenuif Intimare difponimuf
ficut arbitramur ordinato· querere coepim o
tem quafratimiffof apticę fedif&iam adhuc c

Fig.4 Laon, Bibliothèque municipale MS 407, fol. 63r. Bishop Hincmar's personal copy of episcopal epistles with Hebrew writings on the
upper margin. Laon or Rheims, c. 870.

Such an association of learned Jews with Christian clergy or literate royalty is not surprising. 'The scholars of the eighth and ninth centuries', wrote B. Smalley in her renowned work *The Study of the Bible in the Middle Ages,* 'had laid down the two lines, "questioning" patristic authorities, and studying Hebrew, on which medieval exegesis would develop'.[40] That Christian scholars studied Hebrew, inevitably from Jews, consulted Jewish scholars, drew from Jewish sources and even used Hebrew manuscripts, mostly biblical, is widely attested by many Christian exegetical texts as well as Hebrew manuscripts glossed in Latin and Hebrew-Latin glossaries.[41] At the end of the Middle Ages Christian interest in Hebrew sources went beyond biblical exegesis and polemic theology when humanists in Italy and Germany became familiar with other facets of Hebrew literature, such as the Kabbala, and even commissioned copies of various Hebrew texts.[42] But only in England can we find tangible evidence that these interests of Christian scholars involved cooperation between Hebrew and Latin scribes. This striking collaboration is manifested by some dozen bilingual and bi-scriptual biblical manuscripts, mostly Psalters, all of them kept, or formerly kept, in English collections, particularly in Corpus Christi College in Oxford. In these remarkable manuscripts, the majority of which are written from left to right, as a Latin codex, the Hebrew text was usually copied first. The Latin version of the Vulgate or the Gallican, and in some of the Psalters also the Hebraica of St Jerome, was usually written in the margins in parallel columns, and a new Latin translation, known as the *Superscriptio Lincolniensis,* was usually inserted as an interlinear gloss to the Hebrew, attempting to render the Hebrew version literally (*see* Fig. 5). The new translation, at least that of the Psalms, was initiated by Robert Grosseteste, the Bishop of Lincoln,[43] and is assumed to have been prepared by some unknown English Franciscans with Jewish assistance after 1235.[44] In a few other manuscripts, mainly Psalters of English provenance, the Hebrew text alone was copied, accompanied by Latin and French gloss, giving transliterations and French or Latin equivalents of Hebrew words.[45] Some of the bilingual manuscripts display a distinctive and rather peculiar style of

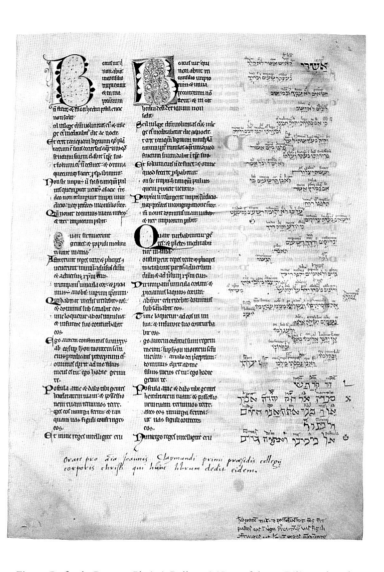

Fig. 5 Oxford, Corpus Christi College MS 10, fol. 2r. Bilingual psalter:
The Gallican and the Hebraica versions of the Vulgate, and the Hebrew
with *Superscriptio Lincolniesis,* England, mid–thirteenth century.

Hebrew Ashkenazic square script, and might have been produced entirely by Christian scribes, though it is hardly likely that non-Jewish scribes were so well trained and qualified in writing Hebrew as to adopt all kinds of intimate scribal and graphic practices (such as devices for producing even left margins and other para-scriptual elements, placement of catchwords and even scribal formulas). The Hebrew texts in other manuscripts are undoubtedly written by typical Jewish hands.[46] Whether the Hebrew in these copies was produced by Jewish converts who were regularly employed by Christian scholars to write Hebrew, as was suggested by Smalley,[47] or by enlisting the services of Jewish scribes, is a matter which cannot be resolved, nor can the question of whether the Hebrew in the other manuscripts was indeed produced by Christians who skillfully and intimately acquired knowledge of Hebrew writing. Whatever the answers to these puzzles, these manuscripts attest to actual collaboration between Hebrew and Latin scribes and to shared book production in thirteenth-century England.

The Hebrew writing in an earlier Hebrew-Latin Psalter from St Augustine's in Canterbury, rediscovered by Lieftinck in Leiden University, and dated to the middle of the twelfth century, was clearly written by a non-Jew in a peculiar and somehow artificial script.[48] However, this entirely Christian manuscript exhibits a striking manifestation of intercultural scribal creativity in some of the initials of its Hebrew text, which were cunningly manipulated so as to playfully represent both the Hebrew and the equivalent Latin letters (*see* PLATE II and Fig. 6).

In a rather similar way, Latin letters were used in a Hebrew manuscript of a later period and different area. In 1420, Gershon ben Hizkiah, a Provençal author and scribe, produced a neat copy of his own work, a rhymed medical manual which he had composed two years earlier while in prison. Only the first two quires of this autograph copy, preserved in the Bibliothèque nationale in Paris, hébr. 1196, were decorated. All the decorated

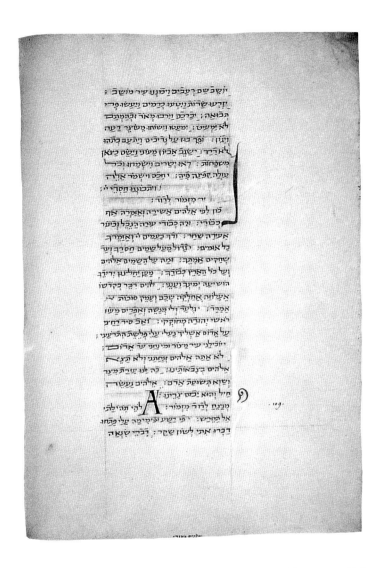

Fig.6 Leiden, University Library MS Or. 4725, fol. 43v. Initials playfully representing both Hebrew and Latin letters, England, mid-twelfth century.

initial words or letters in the first quire are executed in Latin characters, transliterating the Hebrew letters, and two of them were vocalized in Hebrew vowel signs (*see* PLATE III).[49]

The intercultural significance of this unique example of Latin script incorporated conspicuously into a Hebrew manuscript copied by a Jewish scribe is reinforced by the Andalusian type of the Hebrew cursive script, strongly influenced by Arabic calligraphy, which was employed by the author-scribe in Provence, that crossroad of cultures and languages, from where so many Hebrew translations, both from Latin and Arabic, emerged from the twelfth century.

It seems that this manuscript does not demonstrate a cross-cultural phenomenon, but more likely intercultural scribal cooperation. The fact that only one quire was decorated in this way implies that the decorated initial Latin letters were not executed by the Hebrew scribe, but rather by Gentile artists, like the illuminations and illustrations of a considerable part of the illuminated Hebrew manuscripts produced in the West, which must have been made by non-Jewish artists.

To be sure, many illuminated, and most of the decorated, Hebrew manuscripts were executed by Jewish scribes and artists, some of them known to us by name. Their styles, motives and even iconography clearly dominated by those of Arabic decorated manuscripts in the East and Latin illuminated books in the West, and apart from the unique application of elaborate micrography for decorating and illustrating,[50] they do not disclose a distinctive independent Jewish art. But apart from borrowing and adapting the art of illuminating books from the artists around them, it is assumed that Jewish scribes, and mainly those who commissioned or owned books in the West, sometimes entrusted the illumination and particularly the illustration to the hands of Christian artists.[51] Art historians would sometimes not even hesitate to identify the illumination of a Hebrew manuscript as a product of a specific known Christian artist or his atelier.[52]

I should like to refer to two cases which clearly attest to such an intercultural collaboration. The first relates to early thirteenth-century Germany, the second to the late fifteenth-century Renaissance in northern Italy.

Cod. Hebr. 5 of the Bavarian State Library in Munich, a collection of biblical commentaries written in 1232/3, probably in the vicinity of Würzburg, is most probably the earliest illuminated Hebrew codex to have survived from the West. Recently, Robert Suckale has noticed faded instructions for the illustrator inscribed in Latin on the margin of two illustrations.[53] Needless to say such an instruction in Latin must have been intended for a Christian artist. I have recently been able to observe tangible traces left by such a division of production in one of the most spectacular of Hebrew manuscripts, the Rothschild Miscellany, now kept in the Israel Museum in Jerusalem. This stupendous codex, which contains virtually a whole library of some dozens works, biblical, liturgical, halakhic, as well as lay literature, is surely the most extensively illustrated Hebrew book. Written in northern Italy after 1453 and before 1479/80, in Ashkenazic types of script, it was richly decorated and illustrated by hundreds of miniatures. That the artists who executed the illustrations were not Jewish is evident from the vestiges of unusual numbering of the illustrations within each illustrated quire, which must have served as guiding instructions for the artists and perhaps referred to parallel numbering in a model, or was used for the calculation of the artists' fees. While numerals in Hebrew writings, including signatures of quires, are always rendered in the Hebrew alphabetical system, the illustrations in the Rothschild Miscellany are numbered in Indian-Arabic numerals, used in Latin writing. The numbering of prospective or executed illustrations must have been done by a Christian artist, as the surviving numerals in one quire run from left to right, Latinwise. Indeed, in all three miniatures depicting scribes in the manuscript, the scribe is writing from left to right! (Fig. 7). Furthermore, it is possible that even the thousands of initial words were gilded in the same Christian atelier which produced the illustrations. This can be concluded from those cases where the scribe did not notice his own minute marginal inscriptions and failed to execute the initial words or

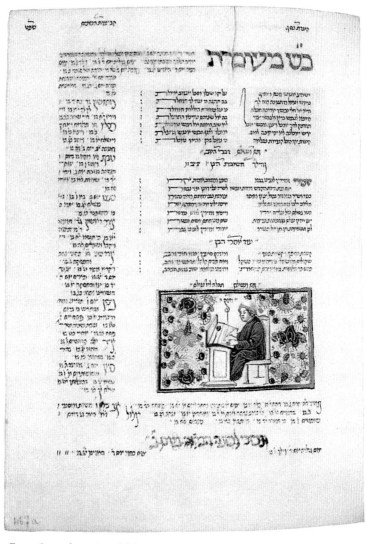

FIG. 7 Jerusalem, Israel Museum MS 180/51, fol. 467r. A miniature of a scribe writing from left to right, Northern Italy, between 1453 and 1479.

22

titles. The missing words were written directly in gold in a crude and untrained Hebrew writing, probably by a non-Jewish decorator.[54]

Let me conclude my introduction by mentioning an entirely Latin manuscript, the Castilian Bible of the Duke of Alba, which mirrors the cross-cultural role which Jewish scholars played in Christian countries. This example does not perhaps represent Hebrew-Latin scribal cooperation as much as Jewish-Christian scholarly collaboration, which produced an actual book. This extraordinary manuscript contains a Spanish translation of the Hebrew Bible and a commentary prepared by Moses Arragel, a Jewish scholar from Guadalajara, who was assigned to this job by the Grand Master of the Order of Calatrava in Toledo, and was assisted by two scholars of the Franciscan Order of Toledo. Arragel completed his translation and commentary in 1430. By rendering this date in his colophon in four parallel eras – the Christian, the Spanish, the Jewish and the Muslim – he echoed the multi-cultural reality of Spain at that time. The present copy is richly illustrated by Christian Toledan artists, but many illustrations betray Jewish exegetical and midrashic elements which must have been furnished by Moses Arragel.[55] In his recent study of the codicological and palaeographical aspects of the Duke of Alba's Castilian Bible, Adriaan Keller has noticed an extraordinary phenomenon, which may disclose the influence of Hebrew writing practice or even the participation of Jewish scribes in the production of the manuscript: the Latin letters are not written as usual on top of the ruled lines, but, like the Hebrew letters, below them![56]

The relationships between non-Jews and Jews, particularly between Western Christianity and Judaism, were often violent, brutal and destructive. Yet they were also culturally fertile, stimulating and enriching, as these examples from the domain of book production attest. In the following lectures we shall discuss further manifestations of sharing and influences in styles of script, codicological practices, and book and text design.

II

The Art of Writing and the Craft of Bookmaking

A NY PRESENTATION of the diversified types of Hebrew script, as well as the making of medieval Hebrew manuscripts, is bound to be related to and shaped by the division of the main civilizations within which Jewish scribes and producers of books were active. Any attempt to classify the various styles and characteristics of Hebrew handwritten books turns out to correspond geographically to the territorial zones of the dominating religions, cultures and scripts at the time of the formation and crystallization of the Hebrew codex around the ninth and tenth centuries.

The distinctive calligraphic and codicological Hebrew traditions cluster in accordance with the three main literate medieval civilizations which flourished around the Mediterranean basin – Islam and its Arabic script, Western Christendom and its Latin script, and Byzantine Christianity and its Greek script. The geographical distribution of those distinctive characteristics corresponds to the geo-political orbits of Islam, the Latin West and Byzantium during the formative periods of the Hebrew codex. The division between the Jewish traditions generally persisted until the end of the Middle Ages, notwithstanding major changes in the encompassing geo-political structure and cultural domination.

Thus, Jewish scribal fashions and practices can be grouped into three basic branches. The first is the branch of writing and bookmaking practised in the territories under Muslim rule in the East as well as in the West, which basically shared the same archetypes of script, ductus and the reed as a writing instrument, and were strongly influenced by Arabic calligraphy and book production. The second branch includes writing and book production in the territories of Western Europe which shared the same archetypes of script, ductus and the quill as a writing instrument, and shows a resemblance to the styles and ductus of Latin scripts and Western booklore. The third is the branch of writing and bookcraft in the areas of the Byzantine Empire before its decline, which seem to have been influenced by Greek script and Byzantine booklore.

Hebrew book script and production under Islamic domination is clearly divisible into two palaeographical and codicological entities, an Eastern and a Western. The Eastern Islamic entity, which we term Oriental, gathers together the Hebrew manuscripts produced in the Near East and Central Asia, within the present boundaries of Iran, Uzbekistan, Iraq, east Turkey, Syria, Lebanon, Israel and the West Bank, Egypt, Yemen and Libya, which, at the time when the Hebrew codex was being formed, were all contained in one political unit under the Abbasid Caliphate. In general, as far as script is concerned, one notices some differences between the eastern part of the Orient and the western one, encompassing Syria, Palestine and Egypt, which may have developed since the late tenth century, when these countries were ruled by the Fatimid dynasty.

Western Islamic Jewish booklore includes the Iberian peninsula and the Maghreb – present Morocco, Algeria and Tunisia – which, with the exception of the northern part of Spain, were under Muslim rule, that of the Umayyad Kingdom in Spain, and of the Aghlabids in North Africa, during the formation period. We designate this Jewish scribal entity by the term Sefardic.[1] The Sefardic type of scripts and codicological practices was not materially changed by later political and cultural transformations in Spain. Not only did the Sefardic book tradition persist after the reconquest of Muslim Spain by the Christians, but, paradoxically, it was adopted by the Jews of Christian northern Spain, after the beginning of the *reconquista* in the late eleventh century. Certainly, there are no extant manuscripts explicitly produced in Christian Spain before the twelfth century to attest to a shift from a non-Sefardic to a Sefardic booklore. However, as far as script can reflect such a shift, surviving documents written in Catalonia before and after the reconquest of Muslim Spain show that up to the late eleventh century their scripts resemble those employed in Hebrew documents from England and in later manuscripts from France and Germany. After the *reconquista* from the end of the eleventh century onwards, their scripts were gradually replaced by the Sefardic types of Muslim Spain.[2]

Moreover, the Christian reconquest of Muslim Spain and the political integration of most of the Jewish communities within the Iberian peninsula brought about the diffusion of Sefardic booklore across the Pyrenees, where it prevailed in the regions of Provence and Bas-Languedoc. Following the political incorporation of a large part of Provence into Catalonia at the beginning of the twelfth century, and the arrival of scholars who fled from Andalusia after the Almohad invasion and the destruction of Jewish centres in the middle of the twelfth century, Provence was incorporated into the Sefardic scribal entity, as it was culturally integrated with Spanish Jewry in general. Consequently, Hebrew manuscripts produced in the entire Iberian Peninsula, North Africa, Provence and Bas-Languedoc in southern France shared the same type of scripts and technical practices of book production in the late Middle Ages.

Though the Oriental and Sefardic entities of the Islamic branch have much in common in graphic style and book design, particularly in their use of parchment codices, each has distinctive types of scripts and entirely different codicological practices. The Eastern zone of the Islamic branch is less influenced by Arabic calligraphy, but shows a stronger affinity to Arabic Oriental techniques, such as methods of processing the writing material, quiring and ruling, and book design and decoration. Both Arabic and Hebrew early booklores, particularly those associated with Koranic and biblical codices, seem to have been influenced by Oriental Christian, Syriac, and perhaps Coptic, practices, but this requires more systematic study.

The parchment of Hebrew manuscripts produced in the Orient is the same glossy parchment used in Arabic manuscripts, with sides equalized by almost completely removing the follicles and grains on the hair side, but remaining distinguishable mainly by the difference in colours.[3] The paper widely used by Oriental Jewish scribes since the eleventh century was, naturally, the Arabic paper produced in the Orient from the second half of the eighth century until the end of the Middle Ages, at which point Arabic papermaking drastically declined and was replaced by cheaper imported Italian paper.[4] Consequently, Oriental Hebrew and Arabic manuscripts share the same types of paper, characterized by the visible effects of the moulding technology of flexible, non-metal wires, glossiness, frequent appearance of two layers stuck together, absence of chain lines, or else grouped chain lines which vary according to regions and periods.[5] Like Arabic manuscripts, Hebrew codices from the Orient were usually constructed of quires of five folded sheets (ten leaves), except for Persia and its surroundings, where quires were usually made of four bifolia (eight leaves). Like Arabic codices, Hebrew parchment manuscripts were ruled with hard point, unfolded sheet by sheet, always on the flesh-side, while many paper manuscripts were ruled mechanically by a ruling-board device, a *mastara,* both techniques not practised outside the Orient.[6]

The Western part of the Islamic branch, the Sefardic grouping, is more strongly influenced by Arabic scripts, particularly in the development of cursive and current modes of writing. In the absence of any codicological study of Arabic manuscripts produced in Muslim Spain and North Africa, it is impossible to know at this stage whether the Sefardic manuscripts shared their technical practices, or whether the Sefardic practices rather drew on or were linked to the techniques of Latin Visigothic manuscripts, as a recent study of their ruling implies. The peculiar ruling technique that prevails in many Hebrew Sefardic parchment manuscripts, that of ruling each pair of successive leaves with hard point (on the hair side),[7] has recently been found to characterize Latin manuscripts produced by Arabized Christians in Muslim Spain and in Toledo after its reconquest by the Arabs in 1085,[8] and apparently also Visigothic manuscripts produced in Christian Spain before the twelfth century.[9]

The other main branch of Hebrew booklore is that encompassed by the territories dominated by Christianity in Western Europe and by the Latin script, prevailing in northern France, medieval Germany, England and Italy. This Jewish scribal branch is clearly split into two entities – that of the areas extending north and east from the Alps, and that of the Italian peninsula.

Though certain variations in the style and shapes of script and in some codicological features can be discerned between manuscripts produced in France and Germany, and apparently also England, they all cluster into one scribal entity which we term Ashkenazic.[10] The consolidated Ashkenazic scribal entity is probably rooted in the Carolingian period, as its wide sphere corresponds, *grosso modo,* to the territories embraced by the Empire of Charles the Great, which unified the continental Catholic countries at the beginning of the ninth century. England was naturally a later insular extension of this continental tradition, as its Jewish population originated mostly in northern France and settled there following the Norman Conquest. Gradual migration of Jews from Germany eastward extended the Ashkenazic scribal entity to central and Slavic Eastern Europe in the late Middle Ages.

Italian manuscripts, as early as the earliest dated ones of the eleventh century, exhibit distinctive scripts as well as scribal and technical characteristics within the Occidental branch of Hebrew booklore. At the time of formation the Ashkenazic script, particularly in the Rhineland, may have evolved from the Italian type, which most probably was imported by the influential Italian scholars who settled there in the ninth century. At a later stage, it is obvious that Ashkenazic styles of script inspired Italian writings. As from the end of the thirteenth century Italian scripts show an Ashkenazic influence, which later extended to some scribal practices as well, following the massive settlement of German and French Jews in northern Italy at the end of the fourteenth century. The peculiar Italian entity within the Occidental branch must also have been forged by the practices and writing styles of the important Jewish cultural centers of Byzantine southern Italy, which flourished particularly in Apulia since the ninth century. Future study of early undated Italian manuscripts may very well reveal their affinity to the Greek script and Byzantine practices of southern Italy.

The Occidental branch, especially the Ashkenazic entity, displays a clear affinity to styles of Latin script, in particular to Gothic fashions. As to technical aspects of book production, it is rather premature to specify the extent of similarity and discrepancy between Hebrew and Latin codices because of the lack of a comprehensive geochronological codicological typology of Latin manuscripts, particularly of the late Middle Ages.[11] However, thanks to the partial characterization of Latin practices, mainly in certain periods and regions, already carried out, it seems that while Ashkenazic manuscripts share with Latin ones the nature of the parchment[12] and the common quiring custom of four bifolia (eight leaves in a regular gathering), their pricking[13] and ruling techniques do not correspond to those of Latin manuscripts. Where they do correspond, as in the replacement of relief ruling by coloured ruling, and particularly the shift from dry point to plummet as a ruling instrument, it is evident that the appearance of such shared practices did not coincide chronologically.

The case of the employment of plummet for ruling is illuminating, since it clearly demonstrates that Jewish scribes indeed borrowed this new technology which was introduced into Latin manuscripts as early as the eleventh century,[14] but after some lapse of time. Though plummet had already been used occasionally in Ashkenazic manuscripts at the end of the twelfth century, it was consistently employed only from the last third of the thirteenth, replacing the relief or blind ruling made by hard point as the regular ruling practice around 1300.[15] That Jewish scribes followed the Latin ones is evident not only from the very lateness of the use of plummet, but from literary sources which show that the new technique had been well known among Jews as early as the twelfth century, but was rejected because of halakhic considerations. As the Pentateuch Scroll, the ritual *Sefer Tora,* has to be ruled according to the Jewish law, the introduction of the plummet as a colour ruling instrument in the Latin West posed a halakhic question as to whether such a ruling technique might be implemented in producing ritual scrolls. This possibility was totally dismissed by German, French and Provençal rabbis.[16] Since the halakhic law of ruling applied to most kinds of texts, the plummet was avoided by scribes when ruling codices, and adopted only much later.

Coloured ruling in ink, which had been practised by Latin scribes since the twelfth century,[17] was never employed by Jewish scribes outside Italy. Only Hebrew manuscripts produced in northern Italy are found to have been ruled in ink, usually the horizontal lines alone, while the vertical boundary lines are ruled by plummet, but not before the 1420s.[18] The characteristics of the quiring, layout and ruling techniques of fifteenth-century Italian Hebrew books fully match those found by Albert Derolez in his comprehensive codicological study of 1200 humanist Latin parchment manuscripts produced in Italy.[19] However, this complete sharing of technical practices and book design by Hebrew and Latin scribes in the same region and time does not necessarily reflect the influence of Latin book production on the Hebrew in Renaissance Italy, or the extent of the well-attested cultural integration of Italian Jewry within Christian society. It is more likely to be the consequence of the commercialization and mass production of ready-made and often pre-ruled quires.

I propose such an assumption in order to explain the striking phenomenon that more than half the dated Italian manuscripts ruled in ink were written in Ashkenazic and Sefardic types of script by immigrant scribes from Germany, France, Provence and Spain, where such a ruling was never used. I suggest it also· to account for the fact that most of the manuscripts produced in Italy by immigrant scribes are constructed in quires of five bifolia (ten leaves), the typical Italian quire composition, hardly practised in Germany and France, and only occasionally employed in Spain and Provence.[20] Such an assumption is indeed confirmed by inventory lists of fifteenth-century Italian stationers, such as that published by Albinia de la Mare,[21] in which ruled quires are explicitly mentioned. Albert Derolez has suggested that this mass pre-ruling must have been executed mechanically by some ruling device,[22] and Peter Gumbert has shown, on the basis of the pricking and the group forms of horizontal lines, that such an instrument, probably a rake, was in fact used.[23]

The third branch of Hebrew booklore, which seems to be represented by a single homogeneous scribal entity, is the Byzantine. In several ways, in its style of writing, various scribal practices and codicological techniques, this entity formed a bridge between East and West, bearing witness to the influence of both major branches of Hebrew booklore. The impact of Greek script and its offshoots, such as early Slavonic and Glagolitic, on styles of Hebrew writing in the territories of the late Byzantine Empire before its decline has not yet been studied. Here again, a distinctive type of script, which is known to us from letters and documents dating from the early eleventh century preserved in the Cairo Geniza, together with character-istic technical habits, persisted despite political changes and the shrinking of the Byzantine Empire. Thus, Hebrew manuscripts produced until the end of the Middle Ages in the areas of the Greek islands and the Balkan peninsula, Asia Minor, Crimea and the western Caucasus display a common type of scripts, book design, graphic and technical practices, and copying formulas.

The lack of early localized Byzantine manuscripts prevents us from knowing whether the codicological features of Byzantine Greek book production in the east and in southern Italy between 900 and 1200, as presented by Jean Irigoin and Julien Leroy,[24] characterized early Hebrew manuscripts as well. The absence of a typological study of later Byzantine book production also prevents the comparison of Hebrew, Greek and Slavic practices. However, the crude pen decorations, particularly the drawings of bizarre birds decorating catchwords which characterize Byzantine Hebrew manuscripts, are very similar to those found in Greek, particularly Balkanic, and Slavonic manuscripts, and imply further shared customs.[25]

Hence, Hebrew medieval booklore may be classified into five main geo-cultural entities: Ashkenazic, Italian, Byzantine, Sefardic and Oriental. Medieval lists or inventories of hand-written books possessed or inherited by private owners, book dealers or synagogues, as early as the eleventh century in Egypt, and in fifteenth-century Italy, where many manuscripts written in non-Italian hands were produced or brought in by German, French, Provençal and Spanish immigrants, explicitly attest that medieval users of books discerned more geographically specific types of script within our consolidated typology. Those book lists refer, for instance, to 'Iraqi script'[26] in the Orient, distinguish between 'German' and 'French' script,[27] and particularly specify regional scripts of the Sefardic zone, namely, 'Maghrebic',[28] 'Catalan'[29] and 'Provençal'[30] writings. We may also notice regional variations of some codicological practices and particularly of writing styles within the overall groupings of Ashkenazic, Sefardic, and Oriental. Yet we still lack systematic studies and a solid methodology which would substantiate differentiation between regional variants of these script types. However, conspicuous local peculiarities of script, and of some scribal practices, fully justify the singling out of two Oriental sub-entities, that of Iran and its neighbours, such as Uzbekistan, which we shall term Persian-type, and that of South Arabia, designated as Yemenite-type.

Before examining the different types of Hebrew book script it is essential to draw attention to a fundamental operational structure of this script. Hebrew medieval script could be executed in three modes or grades: the square, the semi-cursive (or medium) and the cursive. The entirely rectangular forms of most of the letters in the square mode of most types is unparalleled in other Oriental or Western scripts, but may very well be compared to some early species of them: the angular square forms of the Estrangela type of the Syriac script;[31] a certain style of the Ḥijāzī type[32] and the early Kufic type of the Arabic script,[33] particularly that employed in inscriptions;[34] the Greek Capitals or Uncial, particularly the so-called Biblical,[35] and the Latin square Capitals of early Roman majuscule script.[36] The semi-cursive mode can be compared to the Arabic Mashq[37] or Naskhī scripts,[38] or to the *media* grade of Latin scripts, according to Julian Brown's terminology implemented by Michelle Brown.[39] 'Semi-cursive' (or 'medium') is a more appropriate term than the common misleading usage of 'Rabbinic', a term coined by western Christian scholars in the sixteenth century which has persisted to this day.[40]

The fundamentally threefold operational quality of the medieval Hebrew book scripts was already observed and defined in the early twelfth century by one of the greater talmudic scholars in Spain.[41] To some degree it corresponds to the threefold classification of the Latin Gothic script suggested by Lieftinck – the *textualis, hybrida* and *cursiva* levels of execution,[42] and to extended application of this classification to Latin scripts in general, termed *formata, media* and *currens* by Julian Brown.[43]

The three modes were simultaneously employed in most of the geo-cultural entities and types of script. Only in the Sefardic territories did a fully current cursive develop. By the twelfth century, it was already elaborated to such a degree that the Sefardic type of script has to be classified into a fourfold mode – square, semi-cursive, cursive and current cursive. In other types of script, like the Ashkenazic and the Italian, current cursive writing emerged only in the sixteenth century, while the Oriental script never really acquired such a mode, and its development in the post-Middle Ages was the result of the diffusion of Sefardic scripts around the Mediterranean basin following the expulsion of the Jews from Spain and Portugal at the end of the fifteenth century. Following the settlement of expelled Spanish Jews in Italy, and particularly in Greece, the Balkans, Turkey, Syria, Palestine and Egypt, and their intellectual domination, the medieval typology of the Hebrew script was shaken and reshaped under the strong impact of Sefardic scripts on the local ones. Later migrations of many *marranos,* crypto-Jews from Spain and particularly Portugal, to the Netherlands, Hamburg, and southern France, introduced the Sefardic writings even into Ashkenaz. It seems that gradually a new type of scripts evolved all over the Ottoman Empire, a mixture of the Sefardic, the Oriental, and Byzantine types, that may be called an Ottoman type of Hebrew script.

The differences between the modes of each type of script basically involve the number of strokes required in producing the shape of a letter. The letters of the square scripts are formed by many more strokes than those of the semi-cursive ones; those of the cursive scripts are executed by an even smaller number of strokes, while the number of strokes is reduced to one for most letters in the current cursive shapes.[44] However, cursiveness was not always achieved by reducing the number of strokes, but accomplished by quicker writing which combined several strokes without lifting the reed or quill pen. In the current grade of writing, part of one letter or the entire letter would be combined with the following letter, or even several letters, all executed without lifting the pen. Thus, the modes of script were determined by the speed of execution.

Definitions of the modes of each type of script still need further consideration, and clear morphological and quantitative principles for classifying each mode have not yet been forged.[45] Surely, writing is too dynamic, flexible, and artistic a phenomenon to be rigorously classified, especially when it is produced by scribes trained and accustomed to employing several modes. Inevitably, hybrid terminology (such as semi-square) must be implemented to characterize scripts in certain periods and regions, and the application of the 'current' level to all modes seems to be useful.

In general, the square mode, which must have crystallized in the Orient before the tenth century as a calligraphic script for formal copies of the Masoretic version of the Bible, and whose inception can be noticed already in the late formal script of the Dead Sea Scrolls and the Byzantine papyri,[46] was employed in all regions in the production of elegant or deluxe copies, particularly of biblical, liturgical and talmudic texts, or for singling out glossed texts incorporated into commentaries. The cursive mode, which first evolved as an informal script used for private records, drafts and letters, was soon adopted as a book script, mainly in owner–produced copies and compilations. In most books written in semi-cursive scripts, titles, initial words, and *litterae notabiliores,* sometimes also colophons and scribal formulas, were executed in square script.

The threefold execution of Hebrew medieval book script in fact multiplies the number of its types and subtypes, as the shapes of most of the letters in each mode of a type are entirely different from each other. Consequently, the number of distinctive shapes of writing increases to over twenty species, disregarding chronological transformations.

The rich collection of Hebrew manuscripts in The British Library enables us to present the diversity of types of Hebrew book script by illustrations drawn from this collection alone. It also makes it possible to amplify the presentation of the various crystallized species by including some diachronic representation of changing characteristics over a period of time. The affinity between some of these and non–Hebrew scripts may be illuminated by some illustrations selected from Latin, Arabic and Greek manuscripts, mostly from The British Library collections. These affinities are not usually morphological. Scripts may have entirely different shapes of letters and yet display the same or similar style, ductus (the order and direction of executing strokes), proportions, angles, even the same shapes of dominant single strokes which construct different letters in different alphabets. In addition, shared book designs, similar patterns of *mise en page* and *mise en texte* remarkably affect our perception of similarity, regardless of the differences between scripts and the general direction of their execution (right to left in Semitic alphabets, left to right in European ones). As Colette Sirat has suggested, such an impression of similarity derives essentially from 'global vision', or distanced viewing, by which common styles are clearly perceived despite dissimilarities in shapes and other measurable aspects revealed in close scrutiny.[47]

THE 'ISLAMIC' BRANCH

The Eastern Group

Oriental Square script is represented by a tenth-century biblical manuscript (Fig.8a). This formal 'biblical' square script shows affinity to the earlier and contemporary Arabic oblong Kufic script, represented in Fig.8b by a fragment of a Koran of approximately the same format written in a transitional script between the earlier Ḥijāzī and the Kufic,[48] despite the conspicuous difference in the proportions of letters and in word-spacing. While the extended horizontal strokes of rectangular early Kufic script soon dictated the oblong format of the page which characterized most of the Kufic Korans produced in the ninth and tenth century,[49] early Hebrew Oriental biblical codices were, like most of the Ḥijāzī Korans, much larger in format, and the height of the page was always longer, at least slightly, than its width, as in the upright format of the Hijāzī Korans[50] attributed to the seventh and eighth centuries. The proportion of the written space was almost square, so that the squareness of the script matched the *mise en page*. Moreover, while Koranic codices were always written in one column, the biblical manuscripts were usually written in three narrow columns, and only occasionally in two, like Syriac or Greek biblical manuscripts,[51] evoking the appearance of an open rollbook.

Oriental semi–cursive script is represented by a manuscript written in 1190, probably in Baghdad, which exhibits one of the

Fig.8a London, British Library MS Or. 4445, fols. 61v/62r. Oriental Square script, Near East, mid-tenth century.

many variants of this species (Fig.9). This script does not betray a noticeable affinity to Arabic cursive scripts. However, our specimen displays a scribal practice shared by Oriental Arabic and Hebrew copyists, that of writing final words liable to exceed the margins diagonally, in order to produce even lines. This device, much favoured by Oriental Hebrew scribes when employing non-square modes (*see also* Figs. 10a and 13), and particularly by Yemenite scribes who turned it into a calligraphic fashion rather than a functional layout device, must have been borrowed from Arabic scribes. A similar practice can be seen in Eastern Arabic manuscripts written in Naskhī (cursive) scripts as early as the early tenth century,[52] while the semi-cursive Oriental Hebrew script emerged at the beginning of the eleventh century.

Oriental current semi-cursive script is illustrated by a manuscript written in Judeo-Arabic in Alexandria in 1326

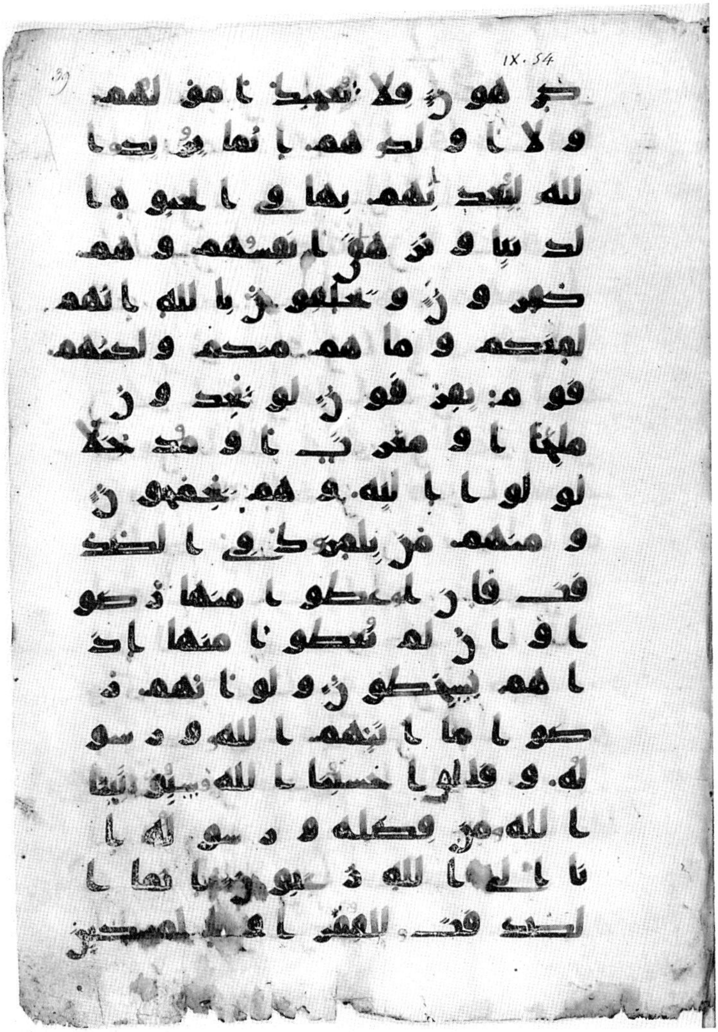

Fig.8b Paris, Bibliothèque nationale MS Arabe 330f, fol. 39r. Arabic transitional script between Hijāzī and Kufic.

שאים אוכר וא עג ראיץ פעלים מעויין עכשו כרמוקמעלרז ·
כסופה אוכר הוא· אבל כרכר שהוא אוס ימתין והוא איט מרנא
לשכור בכרי שכר פועלים אפילו לפי היוקר שעתיקרו שוכר
עליהם פעלים אחדים נותר מכרי שכרו מטעת לוולן· במ
דכריא אמורין ושוכר עליהם כשאיט מוצא לשכור· ואם ומא
כההיא רלעיל הלכו חמריים ולא מצאו תכואה וכול חכבי אוט
דורי ל חייה או אוטו האוו· אם ינע לויותי השוכר לא חוה יהבש
וכול והוא עלה קרו ותו עמו רכפועל כטול הוא רשקל· לא שיימה
קמריה· לא שיימו סוף הכריותא לפעו לאויהבטו לה כלל רמועלאו
גרם· ואויהו הוה לה ל והו נמי למשלוקי אורעתיהן שאם ימצאו שרה
לחה לאדעו מאורתא והולך הטעלים שם וראוה ולא היבט
שהיא לחה·אונשידרו נשמים כלילה· ולומלהן כלל· חאטו וינתהו
ופיהן ועל מנתכק נשכרו ל נהרי לא יכולום ולא היה הלד לד
בכתקי לא שיירוח מאורחת עלו היה לחא לכ ליבר ולחודיוש
אוס התמצאן שרה לחה לו אוקן לכס כלוס ויהיב להן כפועל כטול
פטיר או רפועלים· אונשמים שירדו הפתר פועלם הוא רלוהיכ
להן מירי· אומ להן מגליכן צריס· לא שיירוח פסירו וכל הכות
ראמרו לה מי יימר דארעתא רתהיא ארעו אוגרת· לזוולא לשמוח
שזומ ואוטו מיטרא והשקה אותה ואינה צריכה שר לרולו·
אתא נהרא· גרול הנהר ועלה וככנס כחריצין העשוין·כשרה
ומהביא שותה ואינה צריכה לרוולה אתא נהרא·צ פטירא
רכעל הכות רפועלן אין יורעין כמעהג שרהן שיהו העהר
רגל לעלותולהשקותה אך הוא היה ידע· ופסח עהראמו
משקין אכלשר רמחווא· כמחווא שטם כמקומו שלבבו
הין כע אורא הרגליכ לעאות משנאות תמיר וכשיובכ כטויך רוה
להן יר פועל עלהעלוונה ואפילו הוא חוור כן ריטל לחזר בו

לו גורי שני ל

(Fig.10a). The curviness of some of the extended descending strokes, as well as the cursiveness of some letters produced in one single stroke, can be compared to Mamluk Arabic manuscripts, represented in Fig.10b by a Koran written in large-size Muhaqqaq script in fourteenth-century Egypt.[53]

A fully cursive grade of writing did not develop in the Orient in the Middle Ages, and those manuscripts, and particularly documents found to be written in cursive script were produced by immigrant scribes from North Africa.

Yemenite Square is exemplified by a biblical codex (Fig.11). The squareness of the Yemenite sub-type emerged rather late. Earlier, Yemenite scribes employed either current square script, or a kind of angular, almost triangular semi-square script (Fig.12), which may be compared to the late Eastern bent and triangular Kufic, or the more current slanted semi-square script, which gives the impression of a semi-cursive grade (Fig.13). Both examples are from copies of Maimonides' *Mishne Tora*. Fully semi-cursive or cursive did not really develop in medieval Yemen.

Persian sub-type evolved only in the semi-cursive mode, which is shown in Fig.14.

The Western Group

Sefardic writings form an even more distinctive Hebrew type than does the parallel Arabic type, named Maghribī by Nabia Abbott, a term designating the Arabic script in the Islamic world west (*maghrib*) of Egypt, including Spain.[54] Like the Arabic Maghribī script, the Sefardic type was apparently developed in Tunisia, particularly in Kairouan, then in *Al-Andalus* (Muslim Spain), and later in Morocco and Algeria, while the Andalusian variant rapidly dominated the entire Sefardic zone.

Sefardic Square script is illustrated by two manuscripts produced in Spain – a biblical manuscript (Fig.15) and a deluxe copy of an illuminated Passover Haggada of the late fourteenth century (PLATE IV).

Sefardic semi-cursive script is represented in Fig.16 by a manuscript of the Mishna, written in Agramunt in Spain. Its

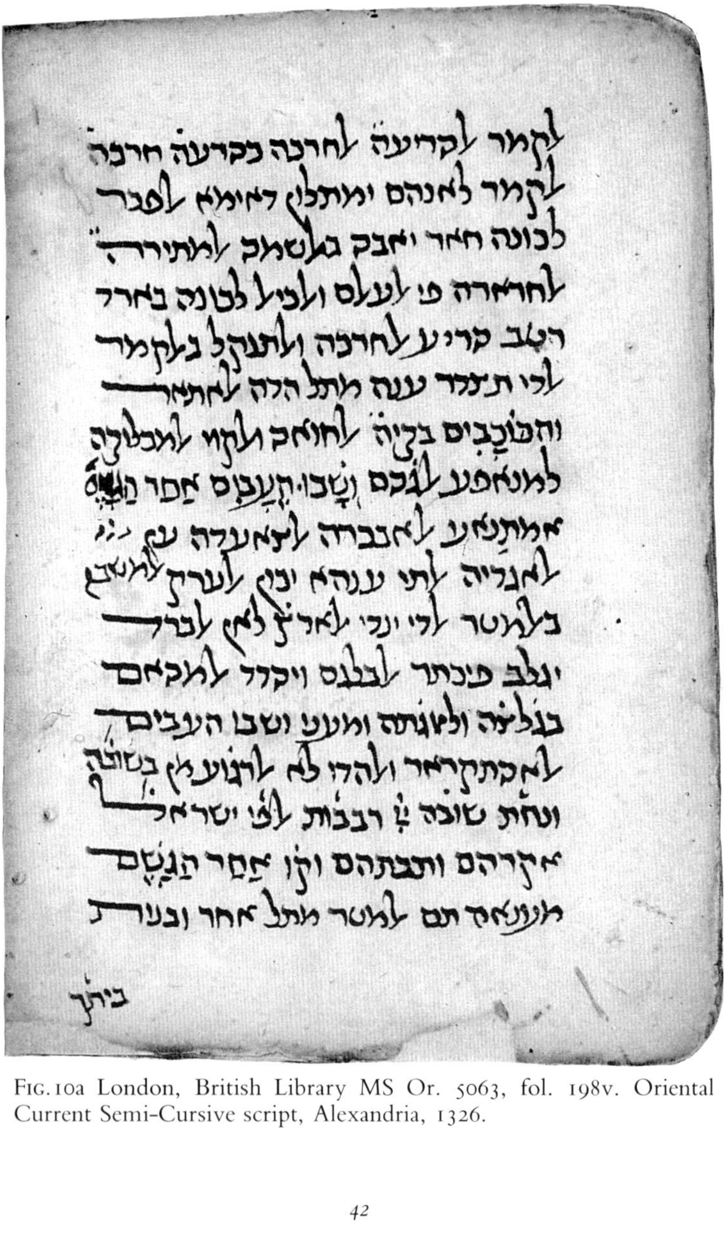

ביתך

Fig. 10a London, British Library MS Or. 5063, fol. 198v. Oriental Current Semi-Cursive script, Alexandria, 1326.

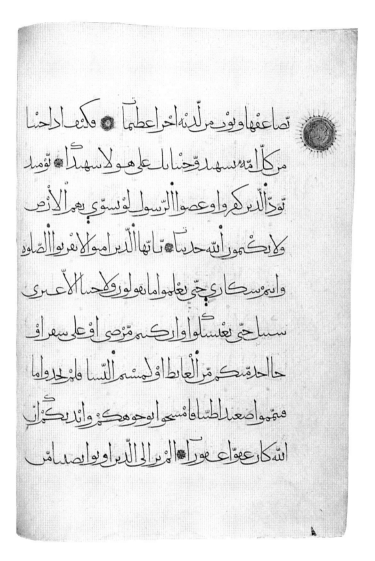

FIG. 10b London, British Library MS Or. 1401, fol. 64v. Arabic
Mamluk Muḥaqqaq script, Egypt, fourteenth century.

Fig. 11 London, British Library MS Or. 1470, fol. 29v. Yemenite Square script, Yemen, 1484.

בבדיה או במד שקל אלא פירצר הוא עשה אומר להנוני מדלא מדלא לי כלי זה

ולמחר נותן לו שוויו ואפלו היה כלי הדיוחר לחדרי ידלאנן והוא שלא

יכול לו שם מדה · סג · הנהתנום חוזר תבלי ומתן לסקריה בשביל

שלא יפסיר מבשיילו אבל האשה לא תמזור חמזר לעיסה וכן לא ימזר

אדם שעורים לפני בהחתו אלא מדשער ומתן לה · סג · ומזותק

לוסדה מן החנוני ביצים ואגוזים במניין וכן כל ביריתא בהזן ובלבד שלא

יכול לו שם דמים ולא סתם מניין פירצר סבום המניין הרי שהיה נושה

בן עשרה לחמבים או עשרה אן אגוזדים לא יאמר ביום טוב תז לי עשרה

כדי שיהיה לך איצלי עשרים אלא לוקח סתם ולמחר עשה השבון

· כד · הולך אדם אצל רועה הרגיל או אצל הטבם הרגיל איצלו ואל בחמה

ולוסה ממנן ועופת כל מה שירצה והוא שלא יזכור לו שם דמים ולא

סבום מניין · כה · הלואת יום טוב תובעין אותה בדין שאם תאמר

לא ניתנה להתבע אינן נותן לו כלום ונדיצא נמנע מישמחת יום טוב

· כו · אעף שיאן מגביהין תרומה ומעשרות ביום טוב כשבת אם

הין לו תרומות ומעשרות שהגביהין מאתמש הרי זה נותנן לכהן ביום

טוב ואין צריך לומד חלה וזדיע ולחיים וקבה שמולוכין בהן ביום טוב

וגבאי צדקה גובין מן הדחצדות ביום טוב ולא יהוא מכלידין כדרך

שמכלידין בחול אלא גובין בצנעה ונותנן לתוך חיקן ומחלקין לכל

שמנה ושמנה בפני עצמה

פרק החמישי

אעף שהותרה הוצאה

ביום פרים אלו שלא ליצוק אכילה לא ישא משאות גדולות כדרך

שהוא

הזֶה עַל הַבָּנִים ה' נִגְלָה הֵיָה הֵיָס זֶה לָקַחַת עַל הַבָּנִים
נִמְצְאוּ כָּל הַמִצְוָות הַנִכְלָלוֹת בְּסֵפֶר זֶה שְׁבָעִים וּמֵהֶם
שְׁמוֹנָה מִצְוֹת עֲשֵׂה וּשְׁתַּיִם וְשִׁשִּׁים מִצְוֹת לֹא תַעֲשֶׂה

סֵפֶר הַפְלָאָה

הִלְכוֹתָיו חֲמֵשׁ וְזֶה הוּא סִדּוּרָן
נְדָרִים הִלְכוֹת נְדָרִים הִלְכוֹת עֲרָכִין וַחֲרָמִין
הִלְכוֹת שְׁבוּעוֹת יֵשׁ בִּכְלָל חָמֵשׁ מִצְוֹות אַחַת מִצְוֹות
עֲשֵׂה וְאַרְבַּע מִצְוֹות לֹא תַעֲשֶׂה וְזֶה הוּא פְּרָטָן א' נִשְׁבָּע
לִשְׁבּוֹעַ בְּשֵׁם ב' שֶׁלֹּא יִשָּׁבַע לַשָּׁוְא ג' שֶׁלֹּא
לְכַפּוֹר בְּפִקָּרוֹן ד' שֶׁלֹּא לְהִשָּׁבַע עַל סְפִירַת מָמוֹן
לְהִשָּׁבַע בִּשְׁמוֹ בֶּאֱמֶת הִלְכוֹת נְדָרִים יֵשׁ בִּכְלָל
מִצְוֹות שְׁתַּיִם מִצְוֹות עֲשֵׂה וְאַחַת מִצְוֹות לֹא תַעֲשֶׂה אֶחָת
שֶׁיִּשְׁמוֹר מוֹצָא שְׂפָתָיו וְיַעֲשֶׂה כְּמוֹ שֶׁנָּדַר ב' שֶׁלֹּא יַחֵל
דְּבָרוֹ ג' שֶׁיָּפֵר הַנָּדֶר אוֹ הַשְּׁבוּעָה וְזֶה הֵן דִּינֵי הֲפָרַת
נְדָרִים הַמְּפוֹרָשִׁין בַּתּוֹרָה שֶׁבִּכְתָב הִלְכוֹת נְזִירוּת
יֵשׁ בִּכְלָל עֶשֶׂר מִצְוֹות שְׁתֵּי מִצְוֹות עֲשֵׂה וּשְׁמוֹנֶה מִצְוֹות
לֹא תַעֲשֶׂה וְזֶה הוּא פְּרָטָן א' שֶׁיְּגַדֵּל הַנָּזִיר פֶּרַע ב' שֶׁלֹּא
יְגַלֵּחַ יְעָרוֹ כָּל יְמֵי נִזְרוֹ ג' שֶׁלֹּא יִשְׁתֶּה הַנָּזִיר יַיִן וְלֹא
תַעֲרוֹבֶת יַיִן וְחוֹמֶץ הוּמִדִין שֶׁלָּהֶן ד' שֶׁלֹּא יֹאכַל עֲנָבִים לַחִים
ה' שֶׁלֹּא יֹאכַל צִמּוּקִים ו' שֶׁלֹּא יֹאכַל חַרְצַנִּים ז' שֶׁלֹּא יֹאכַל
זַגִּין ח' שֶׁלֹּא יִכָּנֵס לְאֹהֶל הַמֵּת ט' שֶׁלֹּא יִטַּמֵּא לְמֵתִים י'
שֶׁיְּגַלַּח עַל הַקָּרְבָּנוֹת כְּשֶׁיַּשְׁלִים נְזִירוּתוֹ הֵן בְּשֶׁיִּטַּמֵּא

הלכות
ג'

Fig.13 London, British Library, MS Or. 10040, fol. 26v. Yemenite
Current Semi-Square script, Ten'im (Yemen), 1338.

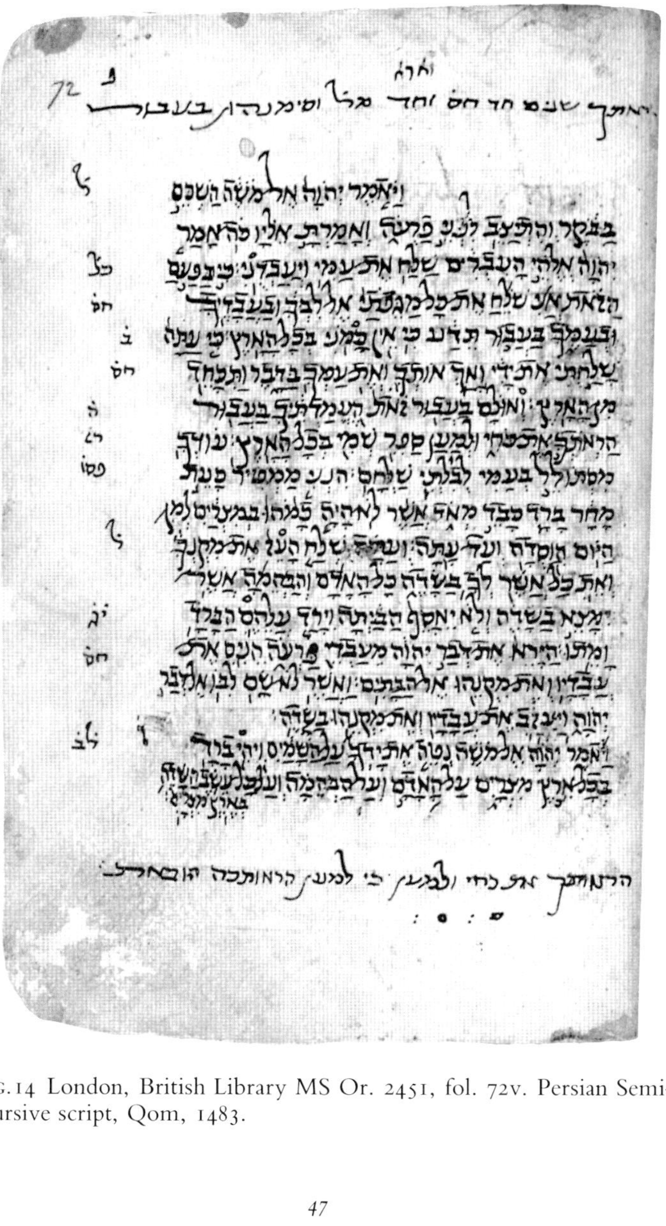

FIG.14 London, British Library MS Or. 2451, fol. 72v. Persian Semi-
Cursive script, Qom, 1483.

Fig. 15 London, British Library MS Harley 5774, fol. 288v. Sefardic Square script, Castelló de Ampurias (Spain), 1396.

48

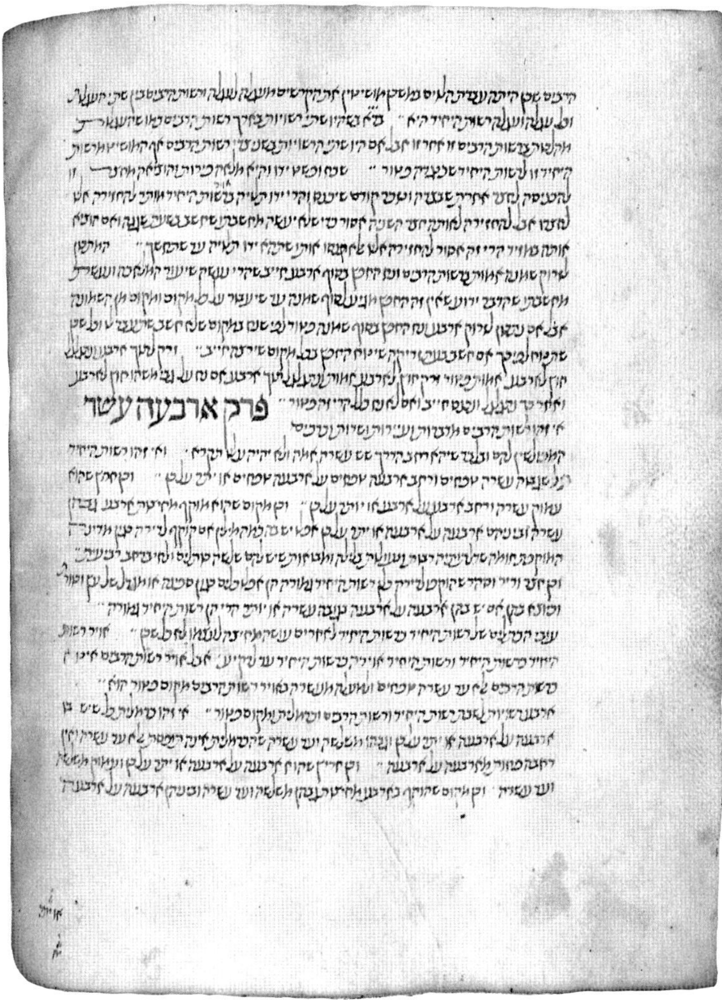

פרק ארבעה עשר

Fig.16 London, British Library MS Add. 17056, fol. 144v. Sefardic
Semi-Cursive script, Agramunt, 1325.

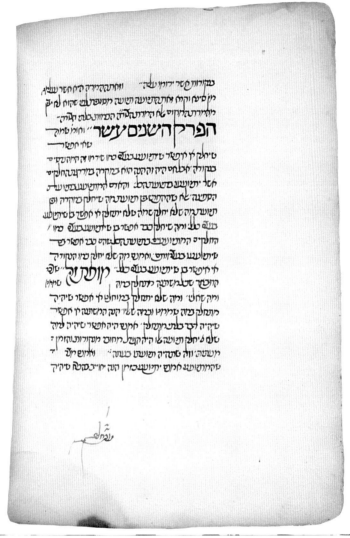

Fig. 17a London, British Library MS Or. 5430, fol. 113v. Late Sefardic Semi-Cursive script, Tunisia? 1476.

Fig. 17b London, British Library MS Add. 11638, fol. 131v. Arabic Maghribī script, Tunis, 1306.

51

later curved and round crystallization, which developed arched extension of the horizontal base strokes under the influence of Arabic script in general, and its round style in Spain and North Africa in particular, is shown in Fig. 17a, written apparently in Tunisia in 1476, compared with an Arabic Koran written in Tunis in 1306 (Fig. 17b).[55]

Sefardic current semi-cursive script is illustrated by a manuscript written in Spain in 1282 (Fig. 18), in which some of the letters, such as *alef, he, qof,* and *tav* are executed by a single stroke and present fully cursive shapes. This contamination of the semi-cursive and the cursive can be defined by the Latin script nomenclature as *bastarda* or *hybrida*.

Sefardic current cursive script – a fully cursive ligatured book hand, noticeably influenced by Arabic cursive script – is represented by a philosophical manuscript written in Spain in 1307 (Fig. 19a). Compare it to an early Arabic Naskhī script (Fig. 19b).[56] Fig. 20a shows a further manifestation of the impact of Arabic script on Hebrew Sefardic scripts. It is a very late offshoot of the Sefardic current writings executed intentionally in imitation of Arabic calligraphy, with excessively elongated elliptical horizontal strokes, or artificially added ornamental extended upward strokes. The opening reproduced is taken from a prayer-book written in the Orient as late as 1815, and shows part of the text of the Song of the Sea (Ex. 15:2–15:15), displayed, as is customary, in prosodic units, separated by wavy strokes, perhaps alluding to the sea waves. The extended basket-like horizontal strokes and the balancing artificial upward verticals can be compared to Fig. 20b, showing an opening from an Arabic Koran, written in Iran in the late nineteenth century.[57]

THE 'CHRISTIAN' BRANCH

The salient difference between the Hebrew scripts of the Islamic zone and those of the Christian zone of the Latin West is basically shaped by the employment of different writing instruments – rigid reed in the former, flexible quill which can produce extreme differences in stroke thickness in the latter – and by the styles of the different dominating non-Hebrew scripts.

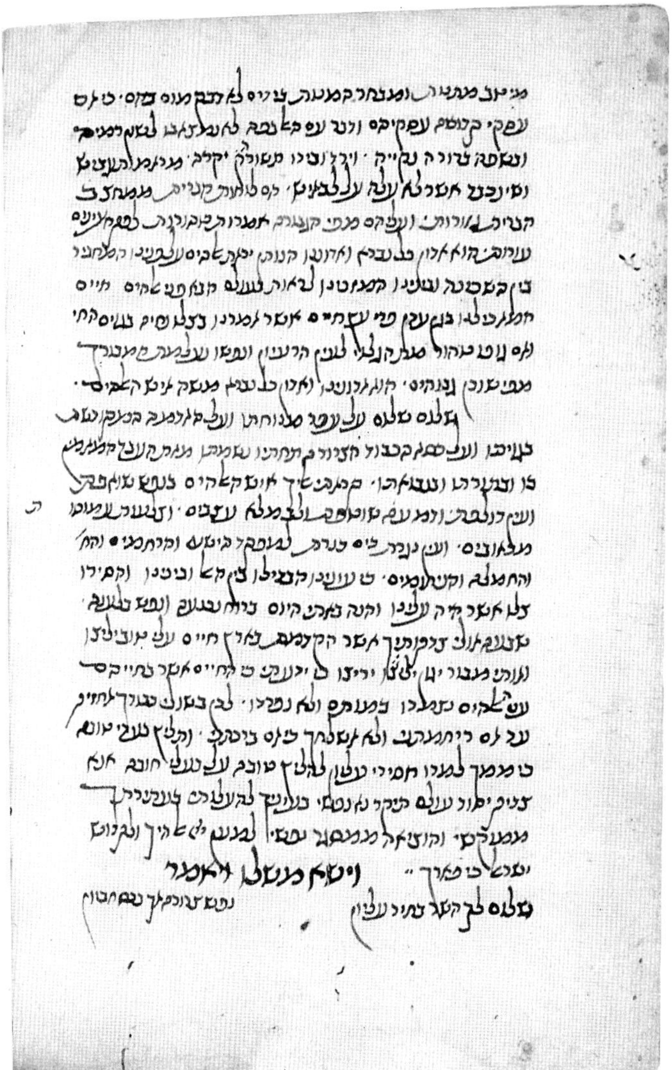

Fig.18 London, British Library MS Add. 27113, fol. 56v. Sefardic Current Semi-Cursive script, Spain, 1282.

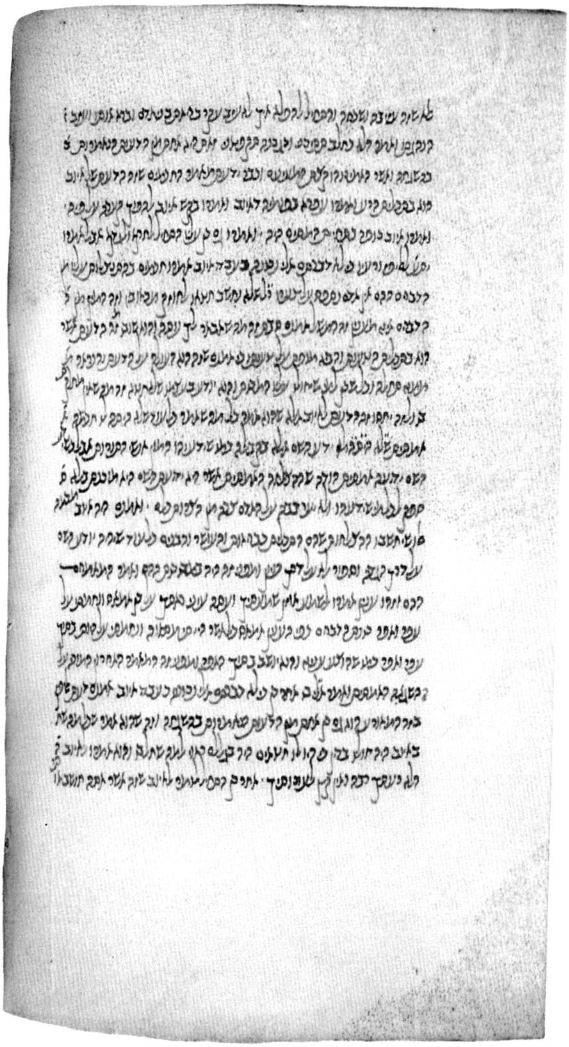

Fig. 19a London, British Library MS Reg 16 A XI, fol. 187v. Sefardic Current Cursive script, Spain, 1307.

Fig. 19b London, British Library MS Add. 7214, fol. 52v. Arabic Early
Naskhī script, Iraq or Persia, 1036.

55

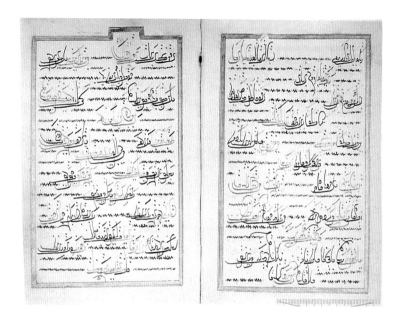

Fig. 20a Jerusalem, Heikhal Shelomo MS 2634. Late Sefardic 'Arabized' Cursive script, Turkey? 1815.

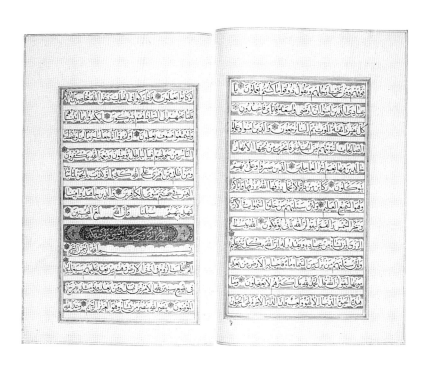

Fig.20b London, British Library MS Or. 12412, fols. 5v/6r. Arabic late
Naskhī script, Persia, late nineteenth century.

57

המלה לפי עינה כי איננה כי אם מגזרת כי נדמה כל
עם כנען ואל תדמו בעבוה לשון גריעה ושביח וכה
פתרון הפסוק לפי עינו אכלב הנביא ההוא ראה
חזירך גדול ומראה מופלאה ונוראה ראה ארץ
אהי יעיר יושב על מארם וניש־א והעינן טלו
ויהי טראותו את המראה הגדול אמר אוי לי כי מ
מית אמות כי המלך יי צבאות ראו עיני מחזה
שדי ראיתי פנים אל פנם לא אחיה עוד כי מות
אמות ובהדאנן על הדבך השיבו אחד מן השרפ
ויאמר אליו אל תירא כי לא תמות וסר עונך וחטאא
תטפר וממו נא הדבר יבין הכי עכיול הלא כה אמר
יעקב בראיותו מלאך יא כי ראיתי א־הים פנם אל פנם
ותנעל עפשי ויא כי לא יראכי האדם וחי וגב מנוח
כה אמר בראיתו המלאך מות נמות כי א־הים ראינו
וגם הנביא הזה אחרי דבריהם נטה ואחז נתיכתכם
כאומרו אוי לו כי נדמיתי ונאספתי כי את המלך
יא צבאות ראו עיני יוכיח על הפתרון כי כן הוא ומ
הבא אחרי ענין כמו טוטה אחורנית לעינין הקודם
לפניו כבו כי א־הים ראיתי כי חטאנו לו כי א־ אליו
הדימנו ירום בענין היה נסרירתי פרצם לטמון
כחיבי עיני יהם טרמונים בארץ וכטמונם במולט
ינמלך מטמון וגבעובונם התפמונה פרנא
נרן ענאך הענא ענו סל הוא פרנם

Fig.22 London, British Library MS Add. 10456, fol. 144v. Ashkenazic 'Gothic' Square script, Germany, 1348.

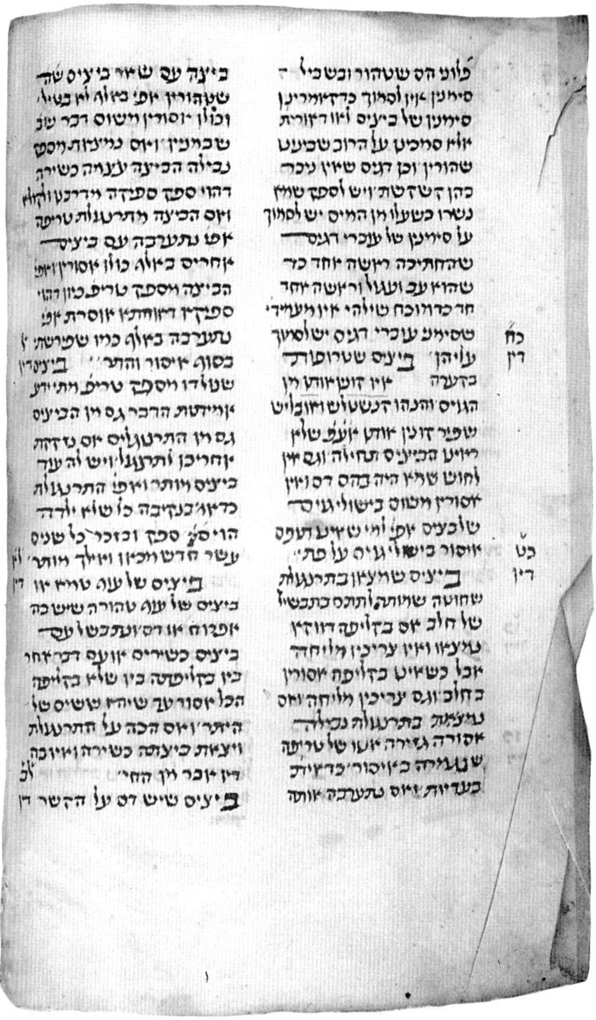

Fig. 23a London, British Library MS Harley 5648, fol. 13v. Ashkenazic Semi-Cursive script, France or Germany, 1253/4.

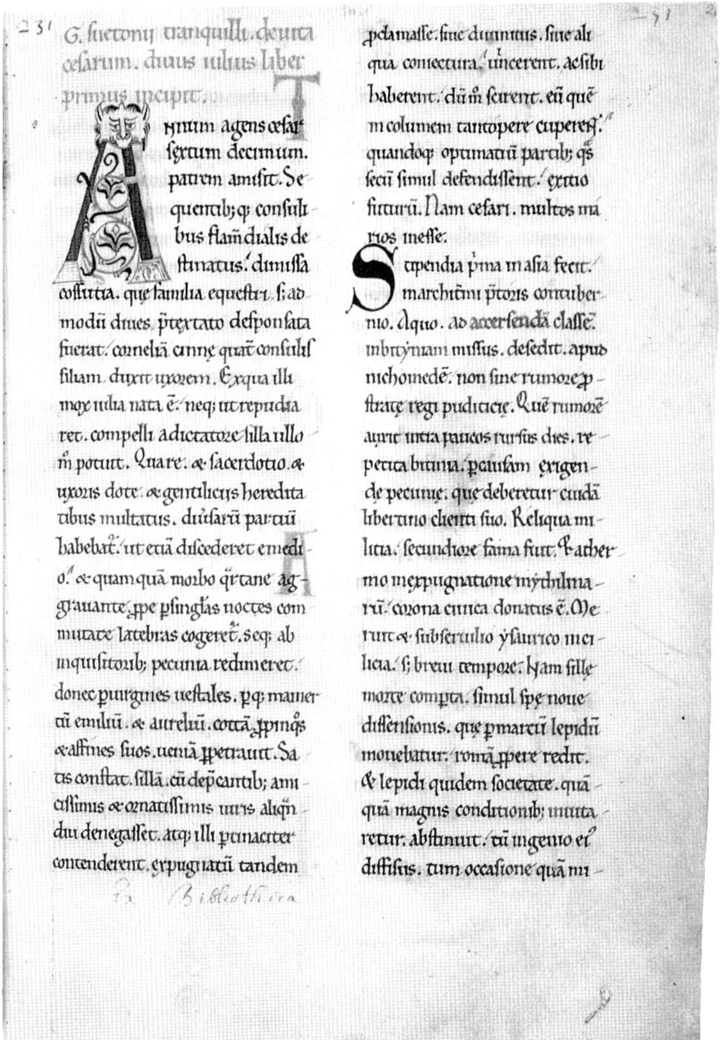

G. suetony tranquilli deuta
cesarum. diuus iulius liber
primus incipit.

ynum agens cesar
sextum decimum.
patrem amisit. Se
quentibz; q; consuli
bus flamdialis de
stinatus. dimissa
costurta. que familia equestri. f; ad
modu dmes. prextato desponsata
fuerat. cornelia cinne qrt cosulis
filiam duxit uxorem. Exqua illi
mox iulia nata e. neq; ut repudia
ret. compelli adictatore filla ullo
m potuit. Quare: & sacerdotio.&
uxoris dote. & gentilicijs heredita
tibus multatus. duaru partiu
habebat. ut etia discederet e medi
o. & quamqua morbo qrtane ag
grauante ppe psinglas noctes com
mutare latebras cogeret. seq; ab
inquisitoribz pecunia redimeret.
donec puirgines uestales. pq; mamer
tu emiliu. & aureliu. cotta ppingos
& affines suos. uenia ppetrauit. Sa
tis constat. silla. cu depcantibz ami
cissimis & ornatissimis uiris aliqn
diu denegasset. atq; illi pcinaciter
contenderent. erpugnatu tandem

pclamasse. sine diuinitus. sine ali
qua coniectura. uincerent. ac sibi
haberent. da m scirent. eu que
m columen tantopere cuperent.
quandoq; optimatiu partibz; qs
secu simul defendissent. erruo
futuru. Nam cesari. multos ma
rios inesse.
Stipendia pma in asia fecit.
in marchitmi ptoris contuber
nio. Aquo. ad accersenda classe.
in bithyniam missus. desedit. apud
nichomede. non sine rumore pp
strate regi pudiciae. Que rumore
auxit intra paucos rursus dies. re
petita bithinia. paufam erigen
de pecunie. que deberetur cuida
libertino clienti suo. Reliqua mi
litia. secundiore fama fuit. & acher
mo inexpugnatione mytilena
ru. corona ciuica donatus e. Me
ruit & subseruilio ysaurico mei
licia. f; breui tempore. Nam sille
morte compta. simul spe noue
dissensionis. que pmarcu lepidu
monebatur. roma ppere redit.
& lepidi quidem societate. qua
qua magnis condicionibz inuita
retur. abstinuit. tu ingenio ei
diffisus. tum occasione qua mi

Fig.23b London, British Library MS Egerton 3055, fol. 2r. Latin
Protogothic script, France, late twelfth century.

Ashkenazic Square script is represented here by two manuscripts. Fig.21 shows an early, pre-Gothic script of a lexical
book written in 1188/9, which seems to suggest Romanesque
style, and has some affinity to Latin Caroline Capitals. Fig.22
displays the Gothic square script of a prayer-book written in
1348 in Germany, in which the flexibility of the quill is fully
exploited, showing an extreme difference between the thin
vertical strokes and serifs and the thick horizontal and widening
curves.

Ashkenazic semi-cursive script is illustrated by a halakhic
manuscript, dated 1253/4 (Fig.23a), which represents a pre-
Gothic, or rather proto-Gothic stage. Its style can be juxtaposed
with the Latin late Caroline minuscule or proto-Gothic book
script, represented in Fig.23b by a French manuscript of the late
twelfth century,[58] of similar layout and proportions in format.

The late Gothic style of the Ashkenazic semi-cursive which
soon evolved under lateral compression, taking greater advan-
tage of the quill's ability to produce extremely varied stroke
widths and moulded by the Gothic sense of verticality, is
illustrated by a halakhic book written in 1394 (Fig.24a). The
similarity between this type of Hebrew script and Gothic Latin
book scripts, particularly the *quadrata* and the *semi-quadrata* and
glossing scripts, is striking indeed, as the comparison with
Fig.24b, showing a thirteenth-century Gothic *semi-quadrata* and
glossing script, reveals.[59] Both large-format manuscripts display
complex pricking and multi-column and additional ruled
boundary lines destined to accommodate the commentary, but
while the partial gloss in the Hebrew book was written on both
margins, that of the Latin, being the major part of the text, is
incorporated within the basic layout. The affinity between the
Gothic Hebrew Ashkenazic semi-cursive and the Latin scripts
can be established not merely by 'global viewing' and the
impression given by the common style and book design, but
also by morphological analysis of letter components.

Ashkenazic current semi-cursive script is represented by
a halakhic glossed manuscript written in Nuremberg (Germany)

in 1391/2 (Fig. 25). While its complex text design recalls the Latin Gothic glossing script illustrated by Fig. 24b, it is more cursive and less Gothic in style.

Ashkenazic cursive script is illustrated in Fig. 26 by a manuscript written in Mestre (Italy) by an immigrant scribe from Germany in 1504. Relatively cursive script had been employed in *Ashkenaz* since the thirteenth century for documentary writings and glosses, but not until the late fifteenth century did it evolve into a fully cursive book hand, showing some similarity to the late German cursive of Latin script.[60]

The Southern Script

Like Italian Latin scripts, Italian Hebrew writings are marked by retention of the Caroline style until the late Middle Ages, while the introduction of the Gothic writing style into Italy had less impact on Hebrew scripts. The dominant rotundity of all the Italian Latin scripts[61] characterizes all the Hebrew scripts as well, particularly the semi-cursive.

Italian Square scripts are represented in Fig. 27, a Romanesque grammatical manuscript dated 1090/1, reflecting the earlier stage which never exhibited a full squareness and may be defined as semi-square script, and by Fig. 28, showing a later development in a philosophical manuscript written in 1283, probably in Rome, by the prestigious scribe Abraham ben Yom Tov ha-Cohen.[62] The influence of the Gothic Ashkenazic style on Italian square scripts, which had already emerged at the end of the thirteenth century but only acquired momentum in the fifteenth century, following the mass emigration of Ashkenazic Jews to northern Italy, can be noticed in the initial words on Fig. 30a.

Italian semi-cursive scripts are illustrated by a philosophical manuscript written in Viterbo in 1273 (Fig. 29a) and by a liturgical manuscript produced in Florence in 1441 (Fig. 30a). While the early stage recalls the Latin, late Italian Caroline Minuscule style (Fig. 29b),[63] the fifteenth-century round crystallization betrays some Gothic aspects which can be compared to Latin Italian Gothic *rotunda* scripts (Fig. 30b),[64] but also calls for a comparison with the Semigothic style of early humanist

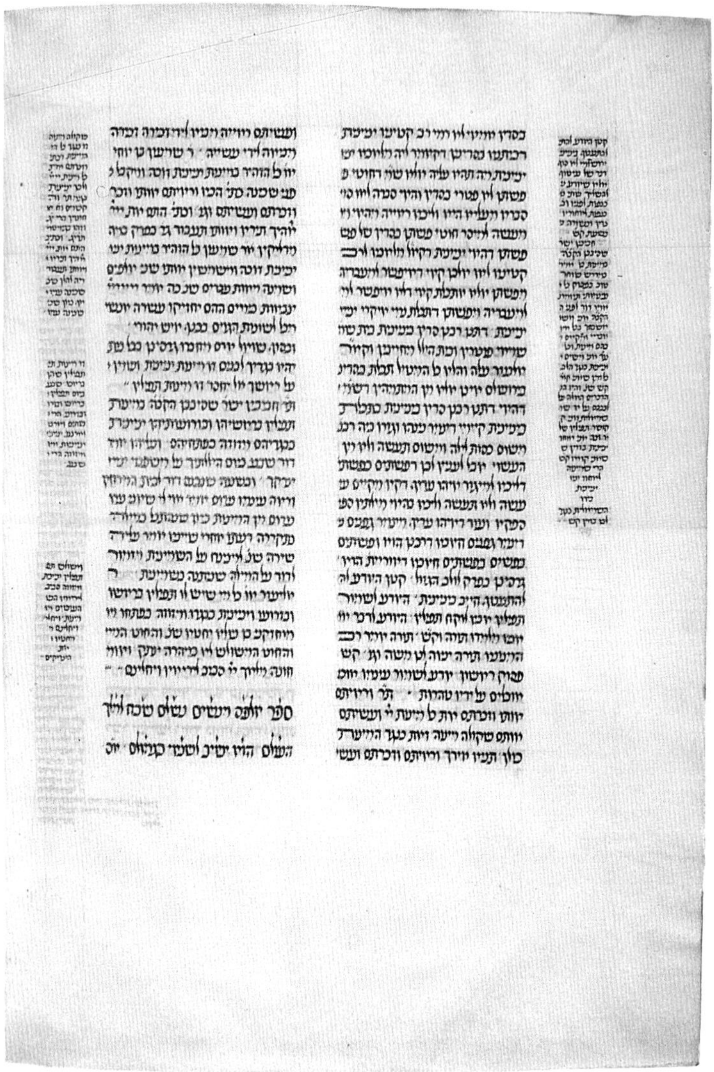

Fig.24a London, British Library MS Add. 17049, fol. 221v. Ashkenazic 'Gothic' Semi-Cursive script, Ashkenaz, 1394.

Fig.24b London, British Library MS Royal 4.E.IX, fol. 170r. Latin Gothic Semi-Square and Glossing scripts, England, mid-thirteenth century.

Fig. 25 London, British Library MS Add. 18684, fol. 77v. Ashkenazic Current Semi-Cursive script, Nuremberg, 1391/2.

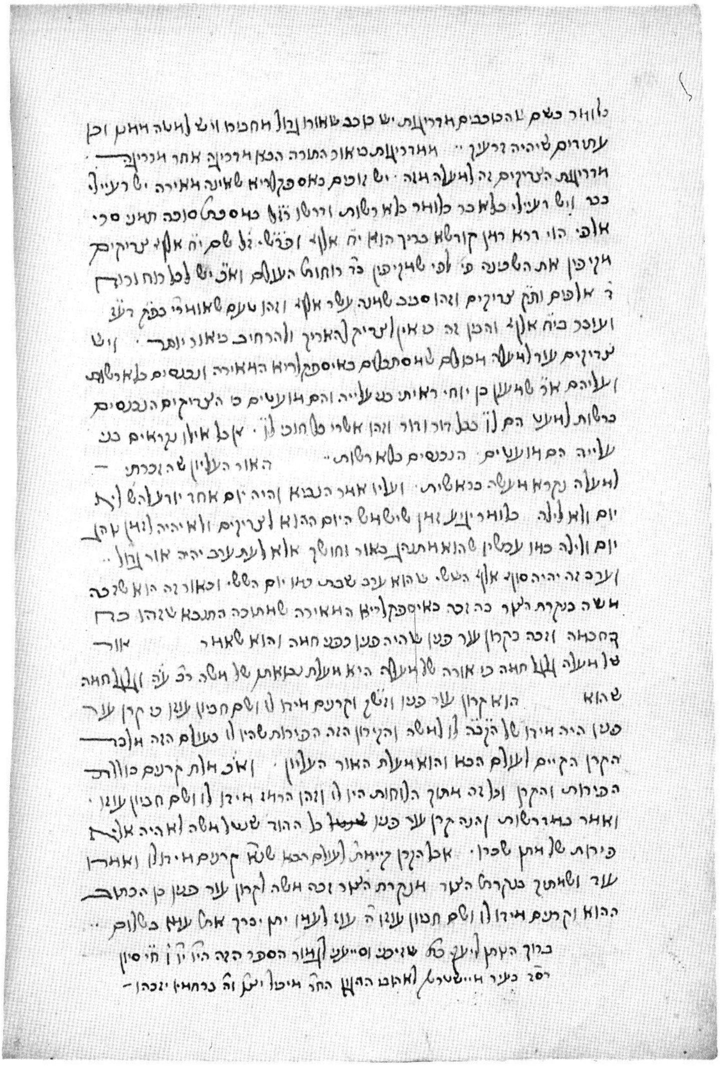

Fig.26 London, British Library MS Add. 27089, fol. 138v. Ashkenazic Cursive script, Mestre (northern Italy), 1504.

ונעצרה ומריה נעשיס כאות שונרפות אותה פצרתי
מאירזת שונרפות מן לכו באור אשכם · טאס לי
אשר אור לו כימון והגור לו בירושלם וכמו ·
מאירות העור מאור · מי גב בכב ויסגר ה
דלהבים ולא האירו מובחי חנם · ולא יתבן להיות
פתרונו כמו יאירו שבעת הנרות הגבה מן
ויאמר אלבים יהי אור ויהי אור · מפני אטר לא
היו שמים הנרות להאיר במזבח · כיראם האש
להעלות עולה ולהקטיר קטרת · והודה לאמת
הגה לו תפארת ואחריך כרכה נשארת ·

לאגורת
והכאת

בחלק אחד לאגורת כסא עם אגרה בקציר מאכלה
וכן לא יראה · כי האגורה היא כגרה זה שונחוותו
מדלה זעני לכבר להב תודה כי מחור הכבר
אגורך · והאגורה והגרך דבם שני שמות משמות
השקלים לשקל אחד אן לשעמס קטנים · זהתבוט
וסור מפחים ויעמס · ולפלט תסובבך רנס ·
עלי עוגב וכנור ומעס · אלוה

ואנו ככבש אלוה יובל לטבח · וכתבת

בספרך כי יהודה בן קורש רסף כפתרון הפסוק
הזה טני זויף האחד במאש אלוה והשני בתוכן
ואין לשניהם דרך לנטוות והמשורבותמר עליו הע
כשברין פתרונו למען כי הוקיה שני הוויב מאלוה
אלה הס אמרת לא יתבן להוסיה זו עלי אלוה · כי
הפמוזים אשר העיד בתוספת הוויב לא ערכם

כרת

Fig. 28 London, British Library MS Harley 7586, fol. 52v. Italian Square script, Italy, 1283.

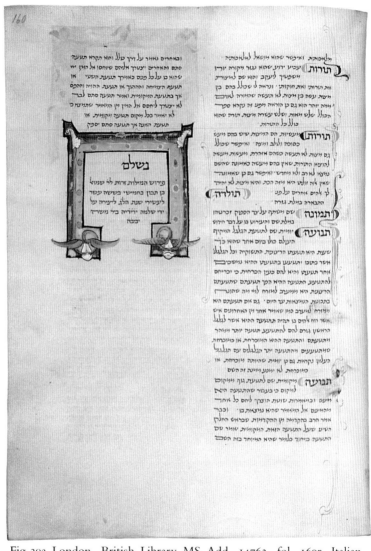

Fig.29a London, British Library MS Add. 14763, fol. 160r. Italian Semi-Cursive script, Viterbo, 1273.

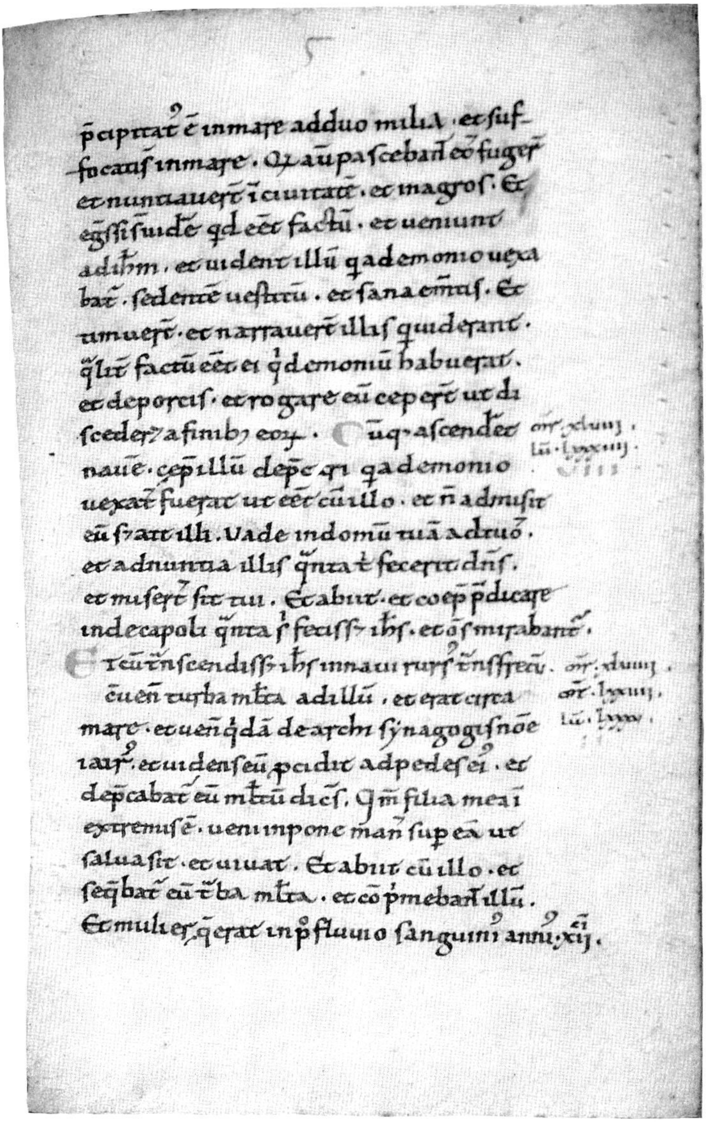

pcipttat ē inmare adduo milia . et suf-
focant̄ſ inmare . Qꝛ aū paſcebant eo fuger̄
et nuntiauert̄ icicuitate . et inagroſ . Et
egſſi ſunt̄ de qd eēt factū . et ueniunt
adihm . et uident illū qa demonio uexa
bat̄ . ſedentē ueſtirū . et ſanac mif . Et
timuert̄ . et narrauert̄ illiſ qui deꝛant .
q̄lit̄ factū eēt ei q̄d demoniū habueꝛit̄ .
et deporciſ . et rogare eū cep ert̄ ut di
ſcederꝛa finibꝰ eoꝛ . Cūq̄ aſcendet̄ oꝛꝛ · xlunj ·
naue . cep illū depe gꝛi qa demonio   lū · lxxxuj ·
uexat̄ fuerat̄ ut eēt cū illo . et n̄ admiſit
eū ſꝛart illi . Uade indomū tuā adtuoſ .
et adnuntia illiſ q̄nta ē fecerit̄ dn̄ſ .
et miſeꝛt̄ ſit tui . Et abiit̄ . et coep p̄dicare
indecapoli q̄nta ſ̄ fecſſſ· ibſ . et ōſ miꝛabant̄ .
Et reuūtnſcendiſſſ· ibſ innaui rurſ tūſſſcū . oꝛꝛ · xluuj ·
cūuen turba mēta adillū . et eꝛat cirta   oꝛꝛ · lxxxuj ·
mare . et ueniꝙ̄ dā dearchi ſynagogiſ noe lū · lxxv ·
iaiꝛ . et ui denſ eū pcidit̄ adpedeſ ei . et
depcabat̄ eū mēta dicſ . Qm̄ filia mei
extremiſ ē . uenu inpone man ſup eā ut
ſalua ſit̄ . et uiuat̄ . Et abiit̄ cū illo . et
ſeqbat̄ eū t̄ba mēta . et cō p̄mebant illū .
Et mulier q erat̄ inp̄ fluuio ſanguini anni · xij .

Fig. 29b Cambridge (Mass.), Harvard College, Houghton Library MS
Riant 20, fol. 69r. Latin late Caroline Minuscule script, Italy, first half
of twelfth century.

71

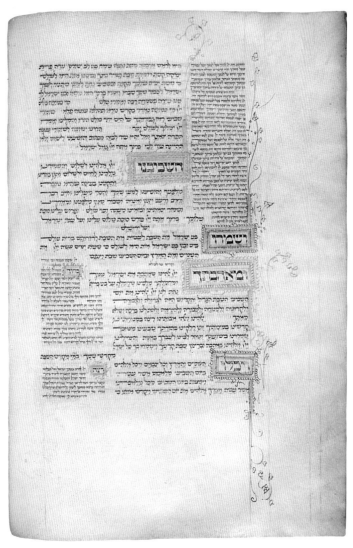

Fig.30a London, British Library MS Add. 19944, fol. 29v. Italian Late Semi-Cursive script, Florence, 1441.

Fig. 30b Cambridge (Mass.), Harvard College, Houghton Library MS Typ 489, fol. 78r. Latin Italian Gothic *rotunda* script, Bologna, late fourteenth century.

73

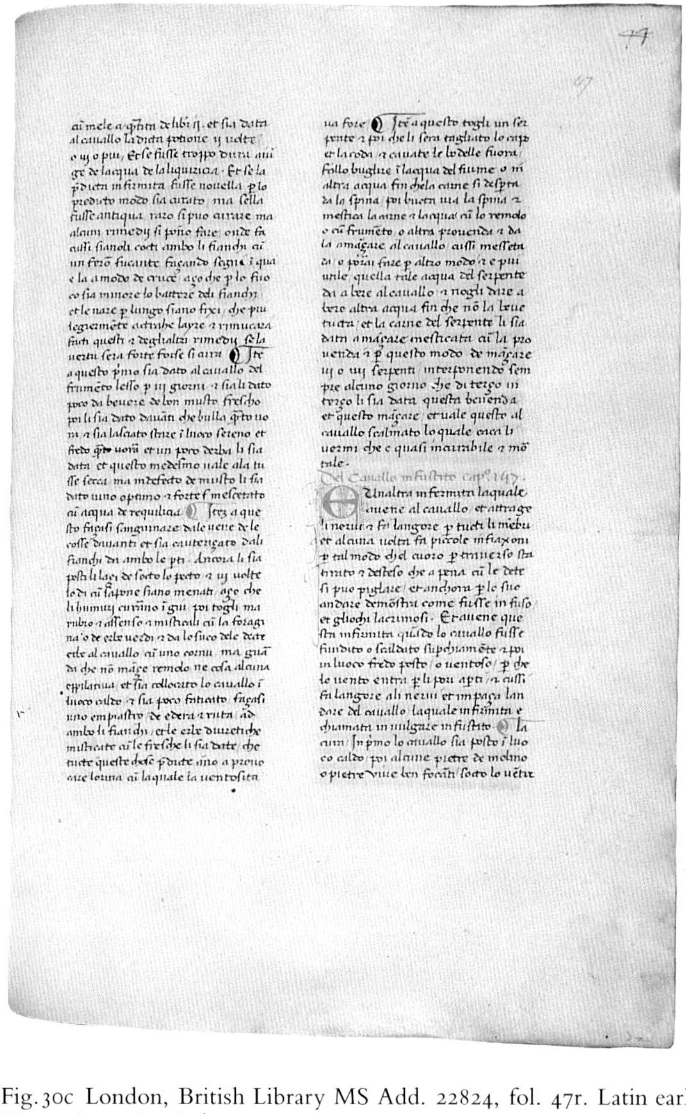

Fig. 30c London, British Library MS Add. 22824, fol. 47r. Latin early Humanist script, Italy, 1422.

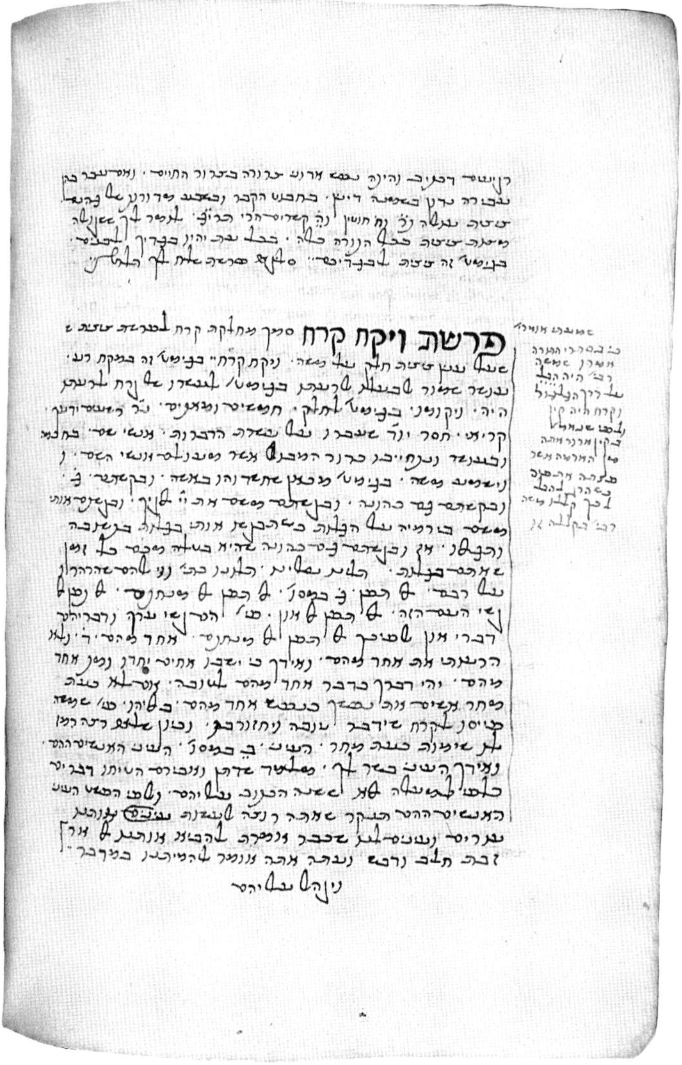

פרשת **ויקח קרח**

Fig.31 London, British Library MS Add. 27034, fol. 76v. Italian Cursive script, Italy, 1530.

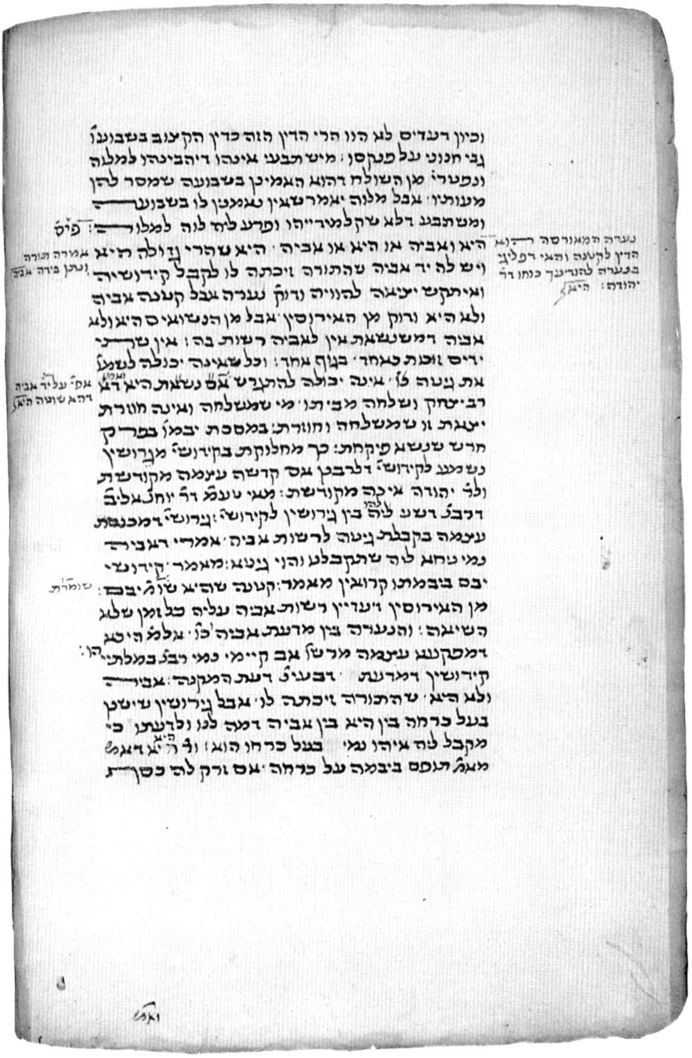

וכיון דעדים לא הוו הרי הדין הזה כדין הקיצוב בשבועו
גבי חנני על פנקסן · מיט תבעי איתהו דיהביזהו למלוה
ונפערזי מן השולח דהוא האמ׳יכן בשבועה שימסר להן
מעונתיו · אבל מלוה יאמר צעין נאמנן לו בשבועה
ומש תבענ דלא איקלמערייהו ופרע לה לה למלוה·ב′ פיס
היא ואביה אן היא אן עביה · היא שהרי זדילך רייג אמרה תורה
ויש לה יד אביה שהתורה זיכתה לו לקבל קידושייה ונתן בידה אבל
ואיתקש יציאה להוייה נדיף עגרה אבל קעגה עביה
ולא היא נדוק מן האירוסין · אבל מן הנשואין היא ונלא
אבזיה דמשתשׁאת. גין לאבזיה רשות בה : אין שׂרי
ירים זוכות כאמר: בגוף אחר: וכל שגינה יכולה לעשׂול
את נעות כלא גיעה יכולה להתגרש שאין עושׂות היא דה
רב יוחק ונשלחה מביתו: מי שמשלחה וגיענה חוזרת
יאגת וו מ מעשלחה וחוזרת: במסכת יבמ′ בפרק ק′
חרש שנשׂא פיקחת: כך מחלוקת בקידועין מברושין
גׁש מעע לקידוש′ דלרבבן אגם קדשה עעמה מקין ורשֹת
ולב יהודה אי כה מקינורשת: מגי עעמא רבֹ יחלם עלא ב
דרבב נשׁע לה בן בירושין לקירושי: בדינש דׁמכנשׂ
עעמא בקבלת גיטה לרשות אביה: אמרי רבבינ
גמי טרוע לה הי שתנקבלבן והני בינשׁא:מאמר קידנעצי
יבם בבמלתו קדואין מאמר: קונעה שהיא שלה יבם
מן האירוסין זיעדיין רישות אביה עליה כל ומן שלא
השיאה: והנעגרה בין מדעת אביה זה′ עלמא היטא
דמכטנשע עעגמה מרעֹל אב קיימי· גמי רב במלתי.הו
קידישין דמדעת · דבעיה דעת המקנה· אבו
ולא היא · שהתורה זיכתה לו אבל בירונשין עישען
בעל כרמה בין היא בין עביה דמה לגן ולדעתו· כי
מקבל לה איהו נמי · בעל כרחי הוא· וב הׁׁרׁ אׁנׂא
מאמ טעפם ביבמה על כרחה ·אם זרק לה כסף ת

Fig.32a London, British Library MS Or. 2891, fol. 61v. Byzantine Semi-Cursive script, Byzantium, 1385.

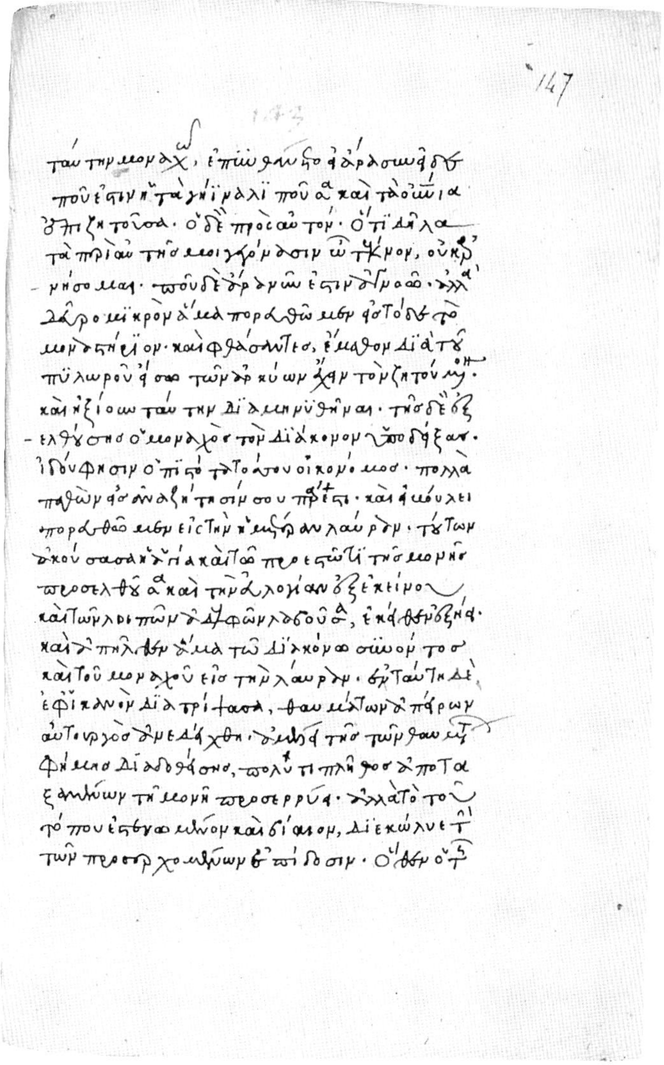

Fig.32b London, British Library MS Harley 5782, fol. 147r. Greek Minuscule script, Byzantium, 1362/3.

writings, represented in Fig.30c by a 1422 manuscript in a similar format,[65] rather than the fully restored Carolingian style of the late humanist script.

Italian cursive script, which developed from the late fifteenth century, is illustrated by a manuscript written in 1530 (Fig.31). This script seems to reflect some affinity with Latin cursive humanist scripts.[66]

Byzantine Scripts

While the square script is clearly related to the 'Islamic' branch of Hebrew writing, the semi-cursive is close to the early Italian semi-cursive, while some late variants reflect a certain Sefardic influence. Cursive grades of script never developed in Byzantium, except for compressed words at the ends of lines.

Byzantine semi-cursive is represented by a halakhic manuscript written in 1385 (Fig.32a). The relationship between this script and late medieval Greek bookhands is not yet clear. However, 'global viewing' of both the Hebrew style and fourteenth-century Greek Minuscule manuscripts, represented in Fig.32b by a manuscript of a similar format and layout written in 1362/3,[67] discloses a certain similarity.[68]

★ ★ ★

The diversification of Hebrew booklore was not a linear process, but rather plurilinear, to borrow linguistic terminology. Despite their distinctive and partially different characteristics, particularly in the Latin West, diverse types of script and codicological practices seem to be related to the encompassing non-Hebrew calligraphic styles and bookcraft fashions more than to each another. Bridged by shared culture, religion and script, separated by different artistic and technological environments, the history of Hebrew handwritten books may thus be depicted both horizontally and vertically.

III

Scribal Re-Making: Transmitting and Shaping Texts

SCRIBES AND copyists transmitted the verbal records of Oriental and Occidental civilizations by reproducing texts and shaping their forms. They were instrumental agents of cultural continuity and revival. The manual nature of reproducing texts composed or edited by known or unknown, mostly past, authors or redactors had an immense impact on the texts transmitted. Due to the erratic circumstances of medieval publication, texts were disseminated at various stages of their creation and revision, and their authors were usually prevented from controlling their vicissitudes. All scribes, whether Hebrew, Arabic, Greek or Latin, were subject to the same unconscious mechanics of copying which inevitably laid many snares and induced unwitting errors. As is well known, the physiological, psychological and mental process of copying presented many pitfalls to exact reproduction and obstructed the best intentions of scribes to adhere to their models. As D. F. McKenzie put it in the first series of the Panizzi Lectures, 'any history of the book . . . must be a history of misreading'.[1] McKenzie refers to the reading of printed texts, but the same applies to medieval copying. Like Latin, Greek or Arabic scribes, Hebrew scribes can be assumed to have generated the same complicated procedure of decoding signs, memorizing the visually perceived series of words, and converting images into phonetic realizations, either vocally[2] or by silent internal dictation.[3] Nevertheless, the social circumstances of Hebrew book production were fundamentally different from those in other cultures, the Latin in particular, resulting in a greater deliberate interference of the scribes in transmission.

The fundamental difference between Hebrew and Latin, Greek and to some extent Arabic book production stemmed from two cardinal factors of medieval Jewish life in the East and West – general literacy and the lack of political power and organization. Literacy in classless Jewish societies extended to all the male members, in contrast to Christian societies of the West and Byzantium where literacy was confined to the clergy, first in monasteries and cathedral schools, then in universities, and in the late Middle Ages reaching also the lay aristocracy, the upper classes and the bourgeois merchants, particularly as regards vernacular languages.[4] The egalitarian system of elementary education, financed and administered by the autonomous Jewish communities, made nearly all male children competent in reading and writing Hebrew, acquainted them at least with the basic religious, liturgical and legal texts, and encouraged further advanced education.[5] The total literacy of Jewish boys in twelfth-century France is indeed attested in Christian sources by a student of Abelard, who claimed that girls were also educated.[6] This widespread Jewish education seems to resemble the system of popular elementary school education in the Islamic world,[7] where literacy was apparently more extensive than in Christian Europe.

The lack of political structure and the vast dispersion over different political entities prevented the emergence of centralized Jewish establishments and religious or secular leadership, despite communal self-government, internal social and juridical autonomy, and the powerful authority of individual sages.

These two factors affected and moulded book production and text reproduction. General literacy and the lack of centralized political or intellectual establishments shaped the individual and personal nature of Hebrew book production and precluded the standardization of reproduced texts.

From the late seventh until the middle of the thirteenth century Latin books were made and kept mainly in the clerical copying centers of monastic multi-copyist *scriptoria* or cathedral schools. Later they were reproduced by university stationers employing the mass *pecia* system, and towards the end of the Middle Ages were issued to a large extent by commercial urban lay ateliers.[8] The books were preserved in royal, aristocratic and ecclesiastical collections. Some Arabic books were produced under the patronage of caliphs who employed scribes and calligraphers,[9] or in research institutes such as *Bayt al-Ḥikma* and *Dar al-'Ilm;*[10] they were kept in royal libraries or mosques, or in the collections of theological schools.[11] Medieval Hebrew books, on the other hand, were not produced, preserved or disseminated by any establishment or upon its initiative. They did not emerge from any religious, academic or lay institutional copying centres, nor were they produced by large-scale commercial enterprises; they were not collected, preserved or made accessible in any public or sectarian institutions, but were privately and individually produced and consumed.

Hebrew medieval books were either produced by professional or semi-professional scribes commissioned by private individuals to copy requested texts, or were made by the users themselves. The recording and systematic study of almost all extant Hebrew manuscripts with dated colophons indicates that at least half of them were personal user-produced books, copied by educated persons for their own needs, and only half, or probably less than half, were written by hired scribes, either professional, or, in many cases, occasional.[12] There are only a very few known instances which explicitly testify to the impersonal production of Hebrew books by professional scribes for chance buyers in the late Middle Ages,[13] but one can assume that undestined copies of popular texts written by known professional scribes were also sometimes prepared in advance for potential buyers or book dealers. Multi-hand manuscripts comprise only nine per cent of dated Hebrew codices. Books written by more than one hand were indeed considered inferior in thirteenth-century Germany.[14] The small quantities of multi-hand manuscripts were not produced at institutional copying centres, or by commercial teams of scribes, but were probably made by single scribes or scholar-copyists assisted by members of their families or by their students.[15] Only some manuscripts produced in the late Middle Ages in *yeshivot* (Jewish religious academies) in Spain and after the expulsion of the Jews in Morocco, by a shared copying of a few students for their masters, and about a dozen manuscripts copied by individual students commissioned by people outside the *yeshiva*,[16] may have echoed the institutional framework of Latin book production. But in general, copies were privately commissioned, individually or personally produced, and privately disseminated, kept and used.

This remarkably high rate of user-produced Hebrew books, reflecting widespread literacy, and the private nature of book production and consumption which seems to be due to the political status of Jewish communities, are the principal distinctive characteristics of Hebrew booklore. They exhibit a fundamental difference from the distinctive features of traditional Latin book production. Yet the same characteristics, arising from different circumstances, would later typify the lay compilations of vernacular texts in the Latin script, which were, as Armado Petrucci has shown, user-produced books.[17] On the whole, book production and text reproduction in the Jewish world seem to share more similarities with those in the Islamic orbits, where many learned men apparently used to copy books for their own use.[18] Notwithstanding the existence of institutional centres of learning and research, numerous public libraries and the extensive commercialization of books through the *warraqīn,* paper and book dealers,[19] the dominant nature of Arabic book production and consumption seems to have been private, boosted by the early introduction of the cheaper writing material of paper.

The individual mode of Hebrew book production had an immense impact on the reproduction of texts and their transmission. While the transmission of Latin texts was controlled, supervised and standardized by the very circumstances of monastic,[20] clerical, university, and to some extent, even commercial lay book production, the reproduction and distribution of Hebrew texts were never institutionalized, no authoritative supervision guided their selection and propagation, and transmission was governed only by the commissioned professional scribes or the learned copyists who reproduced texts for their own use. Encouraged by authors to correct their works, and aware of the unavoidable corruption imposed by the unconscious mechanics of copying, copyists in particular did not view copying as mechanical reproduction, but instead as a critical editorial operation involving emendation, diagnostic conjecture, collation of different exemplars and even incorporating external, relevant material and the copyist's own opinion.[21]

Consequently, many Hebrew manuscripts present texts not only corrupted by the accumulation of unsupervised involuntary copying errors, but also distorted by editorial or even redactoral reconstruction, contamination by different models and versions, and deliberate integration of pertinent texts. What medieval Hebrew copyists did while copying was indeed to deconstruct the text and then reconstruct it. Therefore, many principles and practices of classical textual criticism, such as establishing the genetic relationships between manuscripts, the stemmatic classification of versions, and restoring the original text, are not applicable to Hebrew manuscripts, not only because many of them represent horizontal rather than vertical transmission and different stages of the variable text[22] and provide us with open recensions, like many European vernacular texts, but also because of the possible intervention of learned copyists.

Like the absence of any scriptoral authority over the development of Hebrew scripts, the production of Hebrew books, the transmission of Jewish texts and their dissemination were not subject to any authoritative initiative or supervision, in sharp contrast to ecclesiastical and political control over the development of scripts,[23] book production and text transmission in the Graeco-Latin world.

Hebrew scribes re-made texts not only through critical and unconscious recreation of their verbal essence, but, like Latin,

Greek and Arabic scribes, also by shaping their forms and forging their visual appearance. Scribes of all cultures were entrusted with the effective responsibility of rendering discursive substance in visible non-verbal shapes and patterns, which affected the meaning of texts and their reception.[24] To be sure, the presentation of texts, *mise en page* and *mise en texte,* was not the autonomous outcome of scribal interpretative and artistic creativity. There were other material and social factors which dictated or strongly influenced the visual incarnation of texts, such as available writing materials and their formats, the length of the text and its function, economic considerations, speed of writing, clients' requirements and social status,[25] aesthetic trends concerning page and text proportions,[26] architectural conventions, and the nature of scholarship.[27] However, the role of Hebrew scribes in this structural, interpretative and artistic configuration of texts was much more independent and decisive because of the individual mode of Jewish book production, the high rate of user-produced books, and the lack of a guiding authority over the dissemination of texts.

In determining the form of the physical book, its size and proportions, and in designing the layout of the copied text displayed on the opening of a codex, the Jewish scribes and copyists themselves created the semiotic representation of various types of texts and generated different conventions of meaningful forms for different genres and functions of texts and books. They had an immense impact on the interpretation and reception of texts by their introduction of titles, initial words, running headlines, decorations, illuminations and illustrations, diagrams and tables of contents. By selecting the types and sizes of scripts, paragraphing and sub-dividing, spacing, underlining certain parts or words, or just by using different coloured inks, they determined the hierarchical structure, gradation and legibility of the texts copied.

Furthermore, certain Hebrew texts, like liturgical cycles and prayer books, were virtually created by scribes. The only Jewish liturgical texts circulating in the early Middle Ages were compilations of liturgical poetry, or concise guides. Scribes in various regions not only shaped the compound form of prayer books and liturgical cycles (*see* Figs. 22 and 30a), but selected and compiled their texts in accordance with local rites and practices and rendered their structures coherent. Glossed biblical, talmudic, liturgical and halakhic corpora also emerged as scribal enterprises, unguided and sophisticated, responding to the changing needs of studying and scholarship and at the same time generating them.

The adoption of the codex form by the Jews coincided with the crystallization of the Masoretic version of the Hebrew Bible. Scribes and vocalizers in the Orient were engaged in fixing the biblical texts in codex form and disseminating them on a large scale. The remarkable scope of this production and diffusion has become known to us only recently, following the dramatic accessibility of the rich collections of the Russian National Library (formerly the Saltykov-Shchedrin State Public Library) in St Petersburg, where some two thousand surviving biblical codices, or their fragments, are kept, many of which have been found to date from the tenth and eleventh centuries.[28] The text of these codices, as in those which followed them in all the other regions of the East and West, was accompanied by the Masora, lexical and grammatical annotations pertaining to spelling, vocalization, and accentuation, intended to safeguard the accurate transmission of the biblical text. These complex notations were written in detail in a minute script on the upper and lower margins, while much shorter and abbreviated notations were written between the columns and on the inner and outer margins (*see* Figs. 8a, 11, and 14). At the beginning, the Masoretic annotations were probably written by the scholarly masoretes themselves, as in the case of the famous Aleppo Codex, which was vocalized, accentuated and masoreted in Palestine around 930 by the most important masorete, Aharon ben Asher, himself.[29] Soon after, the complicated task of matching the copying of the annotations to the relevant text, while disposing them in aesthetic patterns, was left to scribes or vocalizers, who as early as the tenth century exploited the secondary text as a decorative device. Later, scribes or vocalizers enhanced this visual manipulation of the Masora still further, sketching not only sophisticated abstract geometrical and floral interlaced ornamentation, as can be seen in Fig. 15, but also elaborate zoomorphic and anthropomorphic images, even illustrations to the biblical text (Fig. 33).[30] The secondary text lost its verbal meaning altogether, and was transformed into a purely visually expressive tool.

Apart from masoreted Bibles, Hebrew scribes produced many other multi-layer books. The production of the principal part of these compound manuscripts reflects great textual creativity in the integration of core texts with commentaries, glosses and scholia, requiring a complex, changing layout and the functional disposition of corresponding texts. A smaller part of these multi-layered books consists of the parallel disposition of disparate texts which were not related at all, or were related but not dependent, and their production seems to have been generated merely by a scribal urge towards the aesthetic and elaborate configuration of the written space on the openings of a codex.

In these non-functional multi-layered manuscripts, all of them produced in Christian Europe, usually two different texts were displayed on the same page in a pre-planned, pre-ruled uniform layout, accommodating one central text framed by another independent text. Fig. 34 shows an opening of a biblical reading corpus written in Ashkenaz in 1215/6. The four central columns of the two facing pages contain the end of the Pentateuch and the beginning of the *Haftarot*, while the marginal columns, which continue along the lower margins, contain the text of the Song of Songs. Fig. 7 represents the double layer structure of the Rothschild Miscellany, which accommodates about fifty disparate texts copied in a similar way. Most of the coupled texts are completely unrelated and were artificially juxtaposed. As the facing pages are disposed as mirror images, most of the openings of the Miscellany display four central columns entirely framed by the additional text.

In neither case was there any textual or contextual reason for the two texts to be copied side by side. It is hardly likely that financial considerations compelled the scribes to economize on space and writing materials by means of this double layer copying, since both manuscripts are deluxe books, as are other

Fig. 33 Toronto, Friedberg Collection, fol. 304v. Germany, 1264.

87

Fig. 34 London, British Library MS Ar. Or. 2, fols. 271v/272r. *Ashkenaz*, 1215/6.

similar manuscripts. Therefore it must have been the compelling scribal quest for form and design which led to this non-functional presentation of texts.

The most intricate creative enterprise of Hebrew scribes, both intellectually and artistically, textually and visually, involved the production of composite glossed texts, which unlike the non-functional multi-layer texts were usually copied simultaneously, page by page.

The amalgamation of biblical texts, their Aramaic translations and the principal medieval commentaries marked a major scribal achievement in the recreation of texts, which facilitated and enhanced scholarship. The production of such corpora, which seems to have begun at the end of the twelfth century in France, Germany and Italy, required the skillful fitting together of two or more texts of different length, disposed on the same page in attractive and easily legible designs. Some of these books were structured in a simpler, uniform layout, as in Fig.35, showing an Ashkenazic illuminated manuscript dated 1347 with the central biblical text written in a square script and the Rashi commentary written in a semi-cursive minuscule script on the outer margin. Fig.24a represents an even less harmonious fitting of isolated marginal glosses to a halakhic text. Usually the matching of variable-sized parallel interlinked texts led to a fairly flexible layout which retained the general structural uniformity of the openings despite the fluctuations in the design of each of the juxtaposed texts. Fig.36 shows a biblical reading corpus produced in the early thirteenth century in France. The multi-layer page contains the end of the Pentateuch, arranged in a central wide column in a large square script, the standard Aramaic translation in a smaller square script on the outer margin, an additional Aramaic version in a minute current semi-cursive script sharing the outer margin and extending below the standard translation, and Rashi's commentary, written in a larger current semi-cursive, which occupies the inner and lower margins. Fig.37 is a page from a biblical corpus produced in Italy by a French scribe in 1327. The text of the Song of Songs is written in a large square script in one narrow column, the Aramaic translation is in a much smaller square script in a wider parallel column, while two running commentaries are written in a minute semi-cursive script – that of Abraham Ibn Ezra on the upper margin and that of Rashi on the outer and along the lower margins. The need to deploy a flexible layout in producing integrated texts produced decorative and figurative dispositions that conveyed both verbal and visual communications. Fig.38 presents an interlaced design of biblical text and Rashi's commentary in an Ashkenazic fourteenth-century manuscript, while a later Spanish example from a manuscript written in Segovia in 1487 (Fig.39) shows the complex presentation of a central text of the Former Prophets and the parallel Aramaic translation on either side, framed by three different-sized commentaries (by Rashi, David Kimhi and Levi ben Gershon) arranged in changing geometrical patterns.

Such composite multi-text presentations undoubtedly facilitated study, though they probably required what Michael

Fig. 35 Cambridge, University Library MS Ee.5.9, fol. 329v. *Ashkenaz*, 1347.

90

Fig.36 Leipzig, Universitätsbibliothek MS B.H.1, fol. 204v. France, early thirteenth century.

Fig. 37 Oxford, Bodleian Library MS Digby Or. 34, fol. 17v. Italy, 1327.

Fig.38 Vienna Österreichische Nationalbibliothek Cod. Hebr. 9, fol.
39r. *Ashkenaz*, fourteenth century.

Fig. 39 Oxford, Bodleian Library MS Kennicott 5, fol. 46v. Segovia (Spain), 1487.

Camille calls 'choreography of reading'.[31] Scribes must have been aware of the confusion that might be caused by reading such complex compilations of texts; hence their employment of column catchwords, designed to guide continuous reading of each component of the concurrently running commentaries or glosses.

Hebrew printing later imitated the variable layout of commentated biblical manuscripts, which, like talmudic texts surrounded by commentaries and glosses, are similarly presented to this day.

The scribal recreation of commentated core texts was of course not an isolated Jewish phenomenon. It was preceded by the presentation of central text and marginal commentaries in Greek manuscripts, as early as the fourth or fifth century,[32] and in Latin manuscripts since the eighth or the ninth century.[33] Different processes of studying and scholarship in Jewish societies stimulated the reconstruction of commentated texts at a much later date.

Comparison of page and text layout, and of proportions in Hebrew and non-Hebrew codices of the same orbit, still demands a detailed study, though their affinities with each other, partly imposed by common writing materials, seem clear. I should like to draw attention to the similarity of amalgamated glossed books of Hebrew halakhic texts produced by Ashkenazic scribes in France, Germany and Italy and glossed Latin Bibles, in terms of their configuration, scholarly motivation and the intellectual process of their creation and organization.

The scribal enterprise of commentated Hebrew Bibles did not resemble the formation of the Latin glossed Bible in the twelfth century. Unlike the scholastic enterprise, their making did not involve the compilation and incorporation of different explanatory notes and exegetical texts. This difference is reflected in the layout. In Hebrew manuscripts, the authorial commentaries were almost always written on the margins of the central biblical text, as in the early glossed Latin books of the Bible,[34] or in

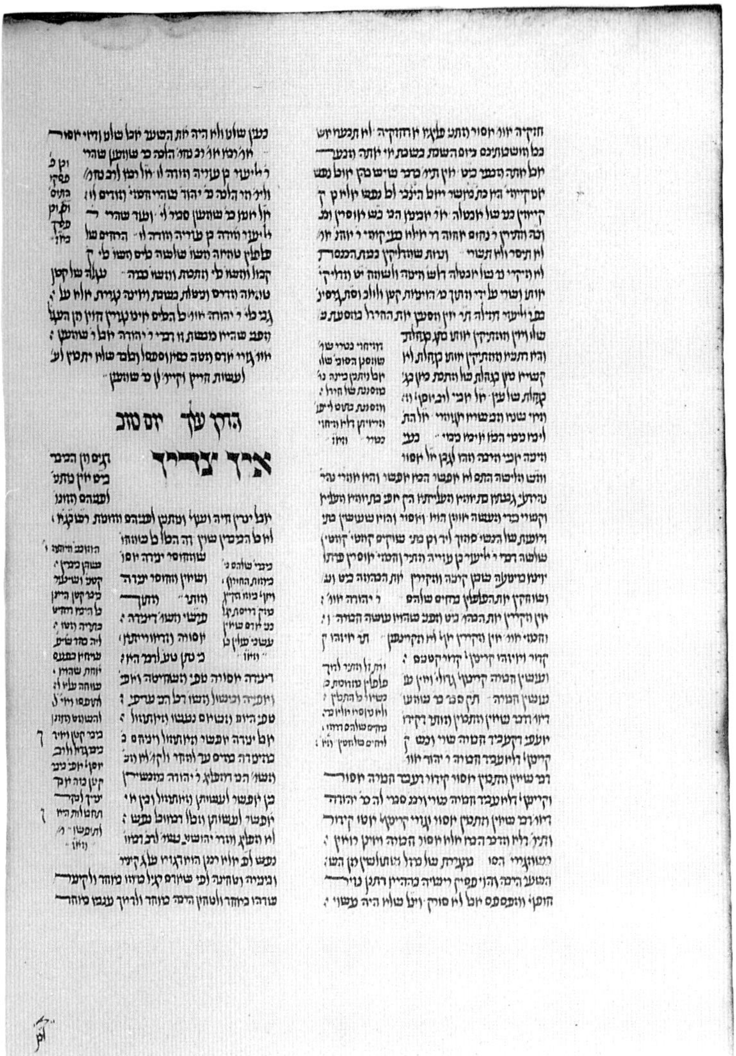

Fig. 40 Paris, Bibliothèque nationale MS hébr. 417, fol. 120v. Germany, 1460.

Fig.41 New York, Jewish Theological Seminary Micr. 8259, fol. 6r.
France, fourteenth century.

97

Carolingian and later commentated Latin texts (compare Fig.30b), and not incorporated within it. The incorporation of the gloss within the biblical text column which marks Peter Lombard's glossed books[35] suited the amalgamation of the exegetical texts. Indeed, when Jewish halakhic creativity declined from the second half of the thirteenth century onward, and compilations and abridgements, glosses, scholia and marginalia replaced cohesive works, a similar incorporated layout was introduced into the glossed books of halakhic corpora.[36] The glosses were not compiled and copied on the margins of the glossed text, but integrated within it. As in Latin glossed books, this integration encouraged the manipulation of decorative configurations, different scripts and splitting of columns.

Figs. 25 and 40 represent halakhic glossed books whose changeable incorporated layout reflects their compilatory nature. Fig.40 shows a page from a glossed abridged talmudic text, whose architectural pattern indeed resembles that of the thirteenth-century Latin glossed biblical text of Peter Lombard shown in Fig.24b. There is perhaps no better demonstration of how meaning affected form than in the intricate and imaginative shaping of the text in MS New York, Jewish Theological Seminary Mic. 8259 (Fig.41), singled out recently by Menahem Schmeltzer.[37] This is a copy of a fourteenth-century prayer book of the French rite accompanied by non-cohesive glosses, notes and commentaries compiled from various sources. The fragmentary nature of the text is reflected by the split presentation of both the liturgy and the incorporated commentaries. Reinforcing the complexity of the layout and its decorative, occasionally figurative effect, the scribe copied on the margins a cohesive unrelated glossed halakhic work which framed the openings of the glossed prayer-book.

It should be noted that the emergence of a variable and flexible layout generated by scholarly developments was associated with a technical change in bookmaking. In Ashkenazic Hebrew manuscripts, and apparently also in Latin codices, this layout coincided with a shift in ruling technique from blind or relief to coloured ruling. While ruling with hard point imposed and guaranteed the uniform layout of at least the two sides of each folio, or usually each bifolium, and even two or more bifolia which were ruled together, the use of plummet, and later ink, for ruling, which had to be applied on each page or each side of the unfolded bifolium separately, enabled changeability of the inner structure of the text design.

Was plummet introduced as a ruling instrument because of the growing demand for complex glossed books, or was it adopted by scribes for some other reason, but encouraged the development of variable layout? To clarify this, and other questions raised while attempting to understand the history of book production, one would have to resort to comparative codicology.

Only comparative study of similar and even disparate codicological features, styles of book script and their changes in different, proximate, confronting or contained cultures can offer us a satisfactory explanation and understanding. Similar practices would prove that they were not conditioned by social or cultural contexts, but were universally structured in the making of a codex. Different practices may be construed by factors other than technological, such as aesthetic conventions or scholarly needs.

A comparative study of book production in societies which employed the codex form should focus first on common technical problems and the ways different cultures resolved them. Different solutions to congruous necessities and diverse technical procedures achieving the same goals would require us to re-examine traditional assertions, extrapolations, and question basic assumptions and premises, including those presented in these lectures. For instance, different quiring practices in different cultures sharing the same writing materials may refute certain explanations of format and quire construction by folding. A comparison of corresponding functional needs and scholarly developments with changes in styles of script, design and manufacture of codices would illuminate the dependence or independence of the changes. Only comparative study of different booklores will enable us to judge whether social or intellectual circumstances entailed those changes, or rather inherent deterministic technical permutations, or whether they were generated by artistic creativity.

Comparative study of different book scripts should concentrate on common structural elements of writing rather than on shapes of letters, as proposed by Jean Mallon with regard to the Roman script:[38] the ductus – the dynamic aspect of executing characters (order and direction of a letter stroke); angle of writing; proportions of height and width of letters, relative 'module', following the modification suggested by Leon Gillissen,[39] and weight – the relationship between the width of horizontal and vertical strokes. It should also examine and compare the relation between book format and text layout and the modular proportions of scripts, attempting to explore whether letter proportions dictated certain formats and layouts, or were influenced by them. Comparative study of scripts may expose common styles of different scripts, and by doing so enrich our ability to analyze and characterize particular scripts.

The necessity of a comparative approach in the study of Hebrew codices whose production was interwoven with other, major and minor, booklores, is self-evident. But the study of the principal codex cultures will surely also benefit from such an approach, which would probably reveal cross-cultural influences and borrowings, particularly in the border regions and multi-scriptual societies around the Mediterranean, such as those of Spain, southern Italy and the Near East, or simply provide us with information contained in one culture's records but pertaining to the history of the book of another culture. I should like to mention two illustrations of the latter possibility, drawn from Jewish sources but referring to the history of paper in Islamic and Christian parts of Europe.

Historians of papermaking and Islamic book production disagree on the date when papermaking began in Muslim Spain. Valls i Subirà, drawing his conclusions from literary Arabic works, declared that it started about 1056,[40] or even earlier, in the middle of the tenth century.[41] Van Koningsveld argued that those texts are late testimonies, unsupported by authentic documents or contemporary sources, and claimed that there are reliable witnesses to the beginning of local papermaking in the middle of the twelfth century.[42] Two authentic Jewish documents of the middle of the eleventh century, letters written in Judeo-Arabic in Hebrew characters found in the Cairo Geniza, refute the twelfth-century dating and corroborate Valls i Subirà's claim. In one letter, the writer informs his cousin, a well-known businessman, that he could not find, as requested, an 'Andalusian' (i.e. of Muslim Spain) paper of good quality, but rather Syrian paper.[43] In another letter by a religious leader and merchant from Palestine, dating between 1050 and 1060, the writer requests a certain halakhic text to be copied for him in Fustat (old Cairo), on high-quality paper, specifying 'not Egyptian paper, but Andalusian or that of Tripoli' (now in Lebanon).[44] Both documents explicitly attest not only that paper was being produced in Muslim Spain by the middle of the eleventh century, but that it had already been exported to the Middle East and had acquired a high reputation there.[45]

The other example is to be found in a halakhic book of legal decisions and responsa by a famous Rabbinic authority, R. Israel Isserlein, compiled by his pupil in the first half of the fifteenth century in Germany. The compiler remarks that his master mentioned at a discussion in the *yeshiva* that in the Gentile courts paper documents were verified by examination of their watermarks. According to Isserlein, documents were sometimes proved to be forgeries when their dates were found to predate their watermarks.[46] In addition to the interesting evidence of a Jewish judicial authority's familiarity with non-Jewish legal system and practice,[47] this Hebrew source testifies to the German practice of dating on the basis of watermarks in the early fifteenth century. I wonder whether there are any similar non-Jewish testimonies.

☆

Bridging East and West, Islam and Christianity, Hebrew handwritten books may indeed serve as a useful means for comparative codicology and palaeography. The marginal Hebrew language and script seem to have been used sometimes as a *lingua franca* for diplomatic communications in the Middle Ages, which Jewish aides in the service of Christian and Muslim rulers might have written and translated upon arrival.[48] Such seems to be the case of the diplomatic epistle sent from the court of 'Abd al-Raḥmān III, the first caliph of Muslim Spain, in Cordoba, to a Byzantine Emperor in the middle of the tenth century. A fragment of a later copy of this letter was preserved in a codex form in the Cairo Geniza, together with another letter addressed to a Byzantine noblewoman, most probably the Empress Helena, wife of Constantine Porphyrogenitus.[49] Both letters were undoubtedly written by Ḥasdai Ibn Shaprut, the leader of the Jewish communities in al-Andalus, who was a highly trusted official at the caliphan court of Cordoba, charged with diplomatic correspondence and negotiations with and missions to European Christian rulers.[50] These letters, as other Hebrew letters by Ḥasdai, were poetically worded, most likely by his secretary, Menaḥem ben Saruq, one of the earliest Hebrew poets and grammarians in Spain.[51] While the epistle addressed to Empress Helena was a private message from Ḥasdai on behalf of the persecuted Jewish communities in southern Italy, the epistle addressed to the Byzantine Emperor might very well have been an official response on behalf of 'Abd al-Raḥmān III to a letter sent by Constantine VII Porphyrogenitus:[52] the fragment includes an explicit acknowledgement of the receipt of an epistle sent by the Byzantine Emperor to "Abd al-Raḥmān, king of Spain';[53] it refers to the Emperor's first-born son,[54] and may have referred[55] to the royal epistle of Constantine VII brought by the Byzantine emissaries in 949, described by the Arab chroniclers as bearing a gold seal with portraits of Constantine [VII] and his son Romanus [II], who was crowned as co-emperor in 948.[56]

As learned Jews, scattered over different countries in East and West, helped bridge language barriers in the Middle Ages, so may Hebrew manuscripts, produced in various Muslim and Christian environments and orbits, furnish common grounds for the study of the codex civilization.

Immersed as we are in the particularities of each script and history of book production, we should embark on a quest for a 'general' or 'universal grammar' of the codex. We should explore the common structural elements, the technical and aesthetic *topoi*, economic and social conditionings, functional and semiotic configurations of texts and iconography of layout which permeate the making of a codex in all the cultures in which the codex performed the magnificent role of propagating texts and knowledge, preserving cultural continuity, introducing new ideas, and inspiring intellectual and social changes. Witnessing the paradoxical and dialectic process of unification and dismantling in our own time, both the tremendous prospects of overcoming political, racial and cultural barriers and menacing national and ethnic fragmentation, historians of the book can humbly contribute to the universality of humankind by promoting a merged, trans-cultural discipline of convergent codicology, and add further common structure and texture to cultural multiplicity.

1 *See* J. Naveh, *Early History of the Alphabet: an Introduction to West Semitic Epigraphy and Palaeography,* Jerusalem 1987, pp.78–112.

2 *See* J. B. Frey, *Corpus Inscriptionum Iudaicarum,* I–II, Città del Vaticano 1936–1952 (volume I was reprinted with a useful and updated prolegomenon by B. L. Lifshitz, *Corpus of Jewish Inscriptions: Jewish Inscriptions from the Third century B.C. to the Seventh Century A.D.,* New York 1975); H. V. Tcherikover et al, *Corpus Papyrorum Judaicarum,* I–III, Cambridge (Mass.) 1957–1964.

3 Cf. C. Sirat, 'Les manuscrits en caractères hébraïques: Réalités d'hier et histoire d'aujourd'hui', *Scrittura e Civiltà,* 10 (1986), pp.247–251 and the referred works.

4 *See* I. Abrahams, H. P. Stokes and H. Loewe, *Starrs and Jewish Charters Preserved in the British Museum,* vol. I, Cambridge 1930; vols. II–III (by H. Loewe), London 1932, and the references in M. Beit-Arié, *The Only Dated Medieval Hebrew Manuscript Written in England (1189 CE) and the Problem of Pre-Expulsion Anglo-Hebrew Manuscripts,* London 1985, p.15 note 4; M. T. Clanchy, *From Memory to Written Record: England 1066–1307,* Cambridge (Mass.) 1979, p.155.

5 *See* M. Beit-Arié, 'Hebrew Script in Spain: Development, Offshoots and Vicissitudes', *Moreshet Sepharad: The Sephardi Legacy* (ed. H. Beinart), I, Jerusalem 1992, pp.283–284 and pls.19, 20, 23. Some of the published documents are written only in Hebrew; their Latin versions must have become detached.

6 *See* C. Sirat, 'Les traducteurs juifs à la cour des rois de Sicile et de Naples', *Traductions et traducteurs au Moyen Age; Actes du colloque international du CNRS organisé à Paris, Institut de Recherche et d'Histoire des Textes,* Paris 1989, pp.169–191. On translations from Latin as well as Arabic, *see* the contribution by J.-P. Rothschild, 'Motivations et méthodes des traductions en hébreu du milieu du XIIe à la fin du XVe siècle' in the same publication, p.279–302.

7 For brief surveys and bibliography on the vernacular languages used by the Jews, *see* the entries 'Jewish Languages', 'Judeo-Greek', 'Judeo-Italian', 'Judeo-Provençal', 'La'az' and 'Yiddish' (*see also* 'Judeo-Persian' for the East) in *Encyclopaedia Judaica,* I–XVI, Jerusalem 1972.

8 *See* the evidence, cited by A. Morris, *A History of Jewish Education,* Jerusalem 1977, p.211 (in Hebrew) on teaching children the Arabic script around 1000 in Iraq (translated into French by Sirat [above, note 3], p.252, note 41). *See also* S. D. Goitein, *Jewish Education in Muslim Countries,* Jerusalem 1962, pp.28; 35; 64 note 42; 135 (referred to by J. Blau, *JQR,* 67 [1976–1977], p.193, note 14). On acquiring the Arabic script as well as possessing Arabic books in Provence, *see* the will of the renowned translator Judah Ibn Tibbon (Granada, *c.*1120-Lunel, *c.*1190) to his son Samuel, in I. Abrahams, *Hebrew Ethical Wills,* Philadelphia 1926, pp.59, and 80. Ibn Tibbon claims that in

Muslim Spain and Christian Provence 'Our foremost men only attained to high distinction through proficiency in Arabic writing' (p.59).

9 In a recent fascinating study P. Sj. van Koningsveld discovered many Arabic manuscripts commissioned or owned by Jews in Christian Spain, and some written by Jewish scribes. *See* 'Andalusian-Arabic Manuscripts from Christian Spain: a Comparative, Intercultural Approach', *Israel Oriental Studies,* 12 (1992), pp.75–110; 'Andalusian-Arabic Manuscripts from Medieval Spain: Some Supplementary Notes', *Festgabe für Hans-Rudolf Singer zum 65. Geburtstag* (ed. M. Foster), Frankfurt am Main 1991, pp.811–823.

10 For example, Maimonides (Cordoba, 1135–Egypt or Palestine, 1204), surely the best known Jewish medieval scholar and author, wrote most of his works in Judeo-Arabic: his influential philosophical book, *The Guide of the Perplexed,* and the treatise on logic, the commentary to the Mishna, *The Book of the Commandments,* medical treatises, and many *responsa.* All his works and part of his *responsa* were translated into Hebrew in the Middle Ages for the benefit of Jewish readers in the Christian countries, some of them already in his lifetime and some in two translations. For a detailed bibliography of Jewish works in Arabic, *see* M. Steinschneider, *Die arabische Literatur der Juden,* Frankfurt a. M. 1902. *See also* A. S. Halkin, 'Judeo-Arabic Literature', in *Encyclopaedia Judaica,* vol. X, Jerusalem 1972, cols. 410–423.

11 *See* J. Blau, *The Emergence and Linguistic Background of Judeo-Arabic,* Jerusalem 1981, pp.34–44; 'R. Nissim's Book of *Comfort* and the Problem of Script in Judeo-Arabic Literature', *JQR,* 67 (1976–1977), pp.185–194. Blau asserts that the bulk of Rabbanite Jewry could scarcely read Arabic characters at all.

12 Cf. G. Khan, *Karaite Bible Manuscripts from the Cairo Genizah,* Cambridge 1990 (*Cambridge University Library Genizah Studies,* 9), pp.1–21 and the bibliography referred to; *idem,* 'The Medieval Karaite Transcriptions of Hebrew into Arabic Script', *Israel Oriental Studies,* 12 (1992), pp.157–176, esp. 159–162. For such manuscripts in The British Library, *see* G. Margoliouth, *Catalogue of the Hebrew and Samaritan Manuscripts in the British Museum,* Part I (London 1899), 189 ff, Part II (1905), 172 ff and R. Hoerning, *Six Karaite Manuscripts of Portions of the Hebrew Bible in Arabic Characters,* London 1889. On additional fragments in The British Library cf. H. Ben-Shammai, 'Some Judeo-Arabic Karaite Fragments in the British Museum Collections', *Bulletin of the School of Oriental and African Studies,* 38 (1975), pp.126–130.

13 To borrow a term coined in literary criticism; cf. G. Deleuze and F. Guatti, *Kafka: Towards Minor Literature* (tr. D. Polan), Minneapolis1986.

14 *See* S. A. Birnbaum, *The Hebrew Scripts,* I–II, Leiden 1971 and London 1954–1957; M. Beit-Arié in collaboration with E. Engel and A. Yardeni, *Specimens of Mediaeval Hebrew Scripts,* Part I, Jerusalem 1987.

15 *See* M. Beit-Arié, Hebrew Codicology: *Tentative Typology of Technical Practices Employed in Hebrew Dated Medieval Manuscripts,* Paris 1976 (reprinted with corrigenda and addenda, Jerusalem 1981).

16 Research has been carried out since 1965 by the Hebrew Palaeography Project, sponsored jointly by the Israel Academy of Science and Humanities (in cooperation with the Jewish National and University Library) in Jerusalem and the Institut de Recherche et d'Histoire des Textes of the Centre National de la Recherche Scientifique in Paris. All the dated manuscripts were traced. Most of them have already been thoroughly studied, and their codicological and scribal features recorded and computerized. The records are processed, retrieved, grouped and correlated by the SFAR-DATA database in Jerusalem. *See* M. Beit-Arié, 'The Codicological Data-Base of the Hebrew Palaeography Project: a Tool for Localizing and Dating Hebrew Medieval Manuscripts', in: D. Rowland and Sh. Salinger (eds.), *Hebrew Studies; Papers Presented at a Colloquium on Resources for Hebraica in Europe*, London 1991 (*British Library Occasional Papers*, 13), pp.165–197.

17 Cf. Beit-Arié, *ibid*, pp.171–173.

18 *See* Beit-Arié, *Hebrew Codicology*, pp.104–109.

19 *See* in detail Beit-Arié, *The Only Dated* etc. (above, note 4), pp.33–35 and plates 6–7; *see* the identification of half of the borrowers by Z. Entin Rokéah, *ibid*, pp.36–56.

20 For a detailed listing of the collections of Hebrew manuscripts, including private ones, *see* User's *Guide: the Collective Catalogue of Hebrew Manuscripts from the Institute of Microfilmed Hebrew Manuscripts and the Department of Manuscripts of the Jewish National and University Library, Jerusalem*, Jerusalem 1989 (attached to a microfiche edition of the catalogue; published by Chadwyck-Healey, France). Since 1950, this institute has been assembling all Hebrew manuscripts on microfilms and cataloguing them, and is about to complete its task. For descriptions of the main collections *see* B. Richler, *Hebrew Manuscripts: a Treasured Legacy*, Cleveland and Jerusalem 1990, pp.138–141.

21 Cf. P. F. Fumagalli, 'Hebrew Manuscripts and Fragments Discovered in Italy', in *Hebrew Studies* (cf. above, note 16), pp.123–129; 'Le copertine ebraiche a Cremona e a Pavia', *Annali della Biblioteca Statale e Libreria Civica di Cremona*, 40 (1989)) (*Studi e Bibliografie*, 4), pp.55–61. Cf. also the series of articles by M. Perani in *Henoch*, 10 (1988), pp.219–234; 11 (1989), pp.103–108 and 363–365; 12 (1990), pp.227–229, and in *Rivista Biblica*, 35 (1987), pp.491–494; idem, *Frammenti di manoscritti e libri ebraici a Nonantola*, Nonantola 1992 (*Archivo Storico Nonantolano*, 1).

22 Colette Sirat, who attempted to estimate the number of books produced by the Jews in the Middle Ages on the basis of historical and literary evidence, surviving inventories of books and demographic estimates of the Jewish communities, arrived at a calculation of one million copies. *See* Sirat, 'Les manuscrits en caractères hébraïques' (above, note 3), pp.260–271.

23 Cf. W. Popper, *The Censorship of Hebrew Books*, New York 1899, particularly pp.6–32. *See also* Sirat, *ibid.*, p.270.

24 Cf. S. D. Goitein, *A Mediterranean Society: the Jewish Communities of the Arab World as Portrayed in the Documents of the Cairo Geniza,* I, Berkeley-Los Angeles-London 1967, p.18.

25 Cf. Turner, *The Typology of the Early Codex,* [Philadelphia] 1977; C. H. Roberts and I. C. Skeat, *The Birth of the Codex,* London 1987; M. McCormick, 'The Birth of the Codex and the Apostolic Life-Style', *Scriptorium,* 39 (1985), pp.150–158; J. van Haelst, 'Les origines du codex', *Les débuts du codex: Actes de la journée d'étude organisée à Paris les 3 et 4 juillet 1985* (ed. A. Blanchard), Turnhout 1989 (*Bibliologia,* 9) pp.13–35. For additional references *see* B. M. Metzger, *Manuscripts of the Greek Bible,* New York and Oxford 1981, p.17, note 32 (the arguments of S. Lieberman, who suggests that the Christian followed an earlier Jewish employment of the codex form, are refuted by the metaphorical usages of *pinax* in talmudic and midrashic literature; cf. Haran, below, note 27).

26 Cf. C. Sirat avec la contribution de M. Beit-Arié, M. Dukan et al, *Les papyrus en caractères hébraïques trouvés en Egypte,* Paris 1985; Beit-Arié, *Hebrew Codicology,* pp.9–10.

27 M. Haran, 'The Codex, the *Pinax* and the Wooden Slats', *Tarbiz,* 57 (1987–88), pp.151–164 (in Hebrew).

28 Cf. E. G. Turner, *The Terms Recto and Verso: The Anatomy of the Papyrus Roll (Actes du XVe Congrès International de Papyrologie,* Part I; *Papyrologica Bruxellensia,* 16), Bruxelles 1978, pp.26–53. For the talmudic sources, *see* S. Lieberman, *Hellenism in Jewish Palestine,* New York 1950, p.206, note 30; A. Sperber, *A Dictionary of Greek and Latin Legal Terms in Rabbinic Literature,* [Ramat Gan] 1984, pp.98–99.

29 *See* L. W. Daly, '*Rotuli:* Liturgy Rolls and Formal Documents', *Greek, Roman and Byzantine Studies,* 14 (1973), pp.333–338; G. Cavallo, *Rotoli di Exultet dell'Italia meridionale,* Bari 1973.

30 Cf. S. Ory, 'Un nouveau type du mushaf: inventaire des corans en rouleaux de provenance damascaine conservés à Istanbul', *REI,* 33 (1965), pp.87–149; J. Sourdel-Thomine and D. Sourdel, 'A propos des documents de la grande mosquée de Damas conservés à Istanbul', *ibid,* pp.73–85. According to the plates, these fragmentary rolls are indeed *rotuli.*

31 Cf. M. Beit-Arié, 'The Munich Palimpsest: a Hebrew Scroll Written Before the 8th Cent.', *Kirjath Sepher,* 43 (1967–68), p.417, note 29; M. Bregman, 'An Early Fragment of *Avot de Rabbi Natan* from a Scroll', *Tarbiz,* 52 (1982–1983), pp.201–222, esp. p.203, note 3 (in Hebrew). Fragments of a Byzantine Hebrew *rotulus,* containing a commentary to the Prophets interspersed with many Greek words and written on both sides are Mss Jerusalem, JNUL 4° 577.7/1 and Cambridge University Library T-S F2(1).211 and K25.288 (I am indebted to Dr Nicolas De Lange for drawing my attention to these fragments).

32 Cf. M. Beit-Arié, 'How Hebrew Manuscripts are Made', in: L. S. Gold (ed.),

A Sign and a Witness: 2000 Years of Hebrew Books and Illuminations, New York and Oxford 1988, p.36; M. Glatzer, 'The Aleppo Codex: Codicological and Paleographical Aspects', *Sefunot*, 4 [19] (1989), pp.260–261.

33 On the authenticity problems of the earliest extant dated Hebrew codex, a copy of the Latter Prophets written according to its colophon in Tiberias (Palestine) in 894/5 and kept in the Karaite Synagogue in Cairo, *see* Glatzer, *ibid.*, pp.250–259. On the refuted early ninth-century dating of another codex of the Latter Prophets, MS St Petersburg, Institute of Oriental Studies D62, which, according to a deed was sold by its owner who had inherited it, allegedly in 847, cf. M. Beit-Arié, *Jewish Studies*, 31 (1991), pp.45–46 (in Hebrew). *See also* the listing of other early codices and fragments, literary as well as documentary, by S. Hopkins, 'The Oldest Dated Document in the Geniza?', *Studies in Judaism and Islam Presented to Shelomo Dov Goitein on the Occasion of his Eightieth Birthday* (ed. Sh. Morag et al), Jerusalem 1981, pp.81–94; 97–98.

34 For details of the earliest extant dated manuscript in each geo-cultural area and the geographical and chronological distribution of the dated manuscripts see Beit-Arié, 'The codicological Data-Base' etc. (cf. above, note 16), pp.169–173; *Hebrew Codicology*, pp.17–19.

35 Most of these translations are listed and discussed in the monumental work of M. Steinschneider, *Die hebräischen Übersetzungen des Mittelalters und die Juden als Dolmetscher*, Berlin 1893 (repr. Graz 1956). *See also* A. S. Halkin, 'Translation and translators (Medieval)', in *Encyclopaedia Judaica*, vol. XV, Jerusalem 1972, cols. 1318–1329. On translations from Arabic to Latin and Castilian and from Catalan to Castilian by Jews in Spain, *see* recently , F. Díaz Esteban, 'Jewish Literary Creation in Spanish', *Moreshet Sepharad: The Sephardi Legacy* (ed. H. Beinart), I, Jerusalem 1992, pp.414–423.

36 Cf. *Catalogue général des manuscrits des bibliothèques publiques des départements*, I, Paris 1849, pp.209–211.

37 Mss Laon, Bibliothèque municipale 407, fols. 63r and 140v. *See* M. Beit-Arié, 'A Hebrew-Latin Glossary – a Testimony of Spoken Hebrew in Tenth Century Jerusalem?', *Tarbiz*, 48 (1978–1979), p.280, note 18 (in Hebrew), and PLATE 1.

38 *See* F. Ravaisson's introduction to the catalogue of the manuscripts of Laon (above, note 36), pp.43–45.

39 On such evidence implied by Charles the Bald himself in one of his decrees, and by Hincmar, who accused Charles the Bald's Jewish doctor of poisoning him, *see* Beit-Arié (above, note 37), *loc. cit.*

40 Third edition, Oxford 1983, p.44.

41 *See* B. Smalley, *The Study of the Bible in the Middle Ages*, esp. pp.338–355, 361–363. On early medieval Hebrew-Latin glossaries *see* M. Beit-Arié, 'A Hebrew-Latin Glossary' (cf. above, note 37), p.276 (an abridged version of the Greek – Old High German – Hebrew – Latin glossary of Ms. Zwettl,

Stiftbibliothek Cod. 1 of the eleventh century is to be found in Ms. Avranches, Bibliothèque municipale 107, fols. 155r–156v), and pp.274–302, in which the so-far earliest known glossary, first referred to by B. Bischoff in *Speculum*, 36 (1961), p.218, is edited and discussed (in Hebrew). The edited glossary, copied in four manuscripts of Latin – Old German glossaries, the earliest dated in the tenth century, includes Latin transcriptions and translations of 29 Hebrew practical phrases and words, probably recorded by a Christian pilgrim from High Germany in the Holy Land. It represents a unique documentation of spoken Hebrew and its pronunciation not later than the tenth century.

42 *See,* for instance, the manuscripts in the Hebrew collection of the Bavarian State Library (M. Steinschneider, *Die hebraeischen Handschriften der k. Hof- und Staatsbibliothek in Muenchen,* Muenchen 1875), Cod. hebr. 72, and 329 (written by a Jewish convert), 103, 112, 115 (written by a Christian) and 31, 32 and 81 (written by Jewish scribes). *See also,* M. Steinschneider, *Vorlesungen über die Kunde hebräischer Handschriften, deren Sammlungen und Verzeichnisse,* Leipzig 1897, p.68.

43 Cf. Smalley, *ibid.,* pp.342–344 and the previous studies referred to, particularly her *Hebrew Scholarship among Christians in XIIIth Century England as Illustrated by some Hebrew-Latin Psalters,* London 1939.

44 *See* the detailed studies of R. Loewe, 'The Medieval Christian Hebraists of England; the *Superscriptio Lincolniensis', HUCA,* 28 (1957), pp.205–252; 'Latin *Superscriptio* Manuscripts on Portions of the Hebrew Bible other than the Psalter', *JJS,* 9 (1958), pp.63–71. Bilingual manuscripts of other scripts are also of great merit for comparative codicology and palaeography. *See,* for example, the Greek-Arabic manuscript in St. Catherine's Monastery in Sinai written there in 995/6 by a Christian scribe who worded his colophon in both languages and scripts; cf. G. Garitte, 'Un évangeliaire grec-arabe du Xe siècle (cod. Sin. ar. 116)', *Studia Codicologica* (ed. K. Treu), Berlin 1977 (*Texte und Untersuchungen zur Geschichte der altchristlichen Literatur,* 124), pp.207–225.

45 Cf. Smalley, *The Study of the Bible,* pp.347–348. On one of these manuscripts, MS Paris, Bibliothèque nationale hébr. 113, a Hebrew Psalter partially glossed in French and Latin, *see* recently M. Garel, *D'une main forte: manuscrits hébreux des collections françaises* [a catalogue of an exhibition at the Bibliothèque nationale, 17 October 1991–15 January 1992], Paris 1991, pp.90–91, n° 60. Garel has noticed the similarity of its script to that of MS Valmadonna 1, a Pentateuch which was written in 1189 and whose English provenance I have tried to establish on codicological grounds as well as by a few Anglo-Norman French glosses written by its vocalizor (cf. Beit-Arié, *The only Dated Medieval Hebrew Manuscript Written in England,* London 1985). Garel also noted in MS Paris notes written in Old English and the Runic alphabet, and observed insular characteristics in the colours of the decoration.

Like other glossed manuscripts which contain only the Hebrew text and are written from right to left Hebrew-wise in a typical Jewish hand, this manuscript seems to have been produced in a Jewish environment for Jewish use and only later to have passed into Christian hands. However, the hybrid numeration of the psalms may very well imply, as Garel suggests, that it was originally commissioned by a Christian scholar or establishment.

46 Cf. Beit-Arié, *ibid.*, pp.7–9 and 21–23.

47 Smalley, *ibid.*, pp.347–348.

48 MS Leiden, University Library Or. 4725; *see* G. I. Lieftinck, 'The "Psalterium hebraycum" from St Augustine's Canterbury Rediscovered in the Scaliger Bequest at Leiden', *Transactions of the Cambridge Bibliographical Society,* 2 (1955), pp.97–104. The Latin version and an abridged *Breviarium in Psalmos* were copied in parallel marginal columns only until fol. 18v and partially also on a few other pages. That the Hebrew was written by a Christian hand was already suspected by M. Steinschneider in his catalogue of the Hebrew manuscripts of Leiden, *Catalogus Codicum Hebraeorum Bibliothecae Academiae Lugduno-Batavae, Lugduni-Batavorum* 1858, MS Scal. 8, p.349. On a twelfth-century Spanish (?) polyglot Psalter which contains the Hebrew, Greek and two Latin versions written in parallel columns, also kept in Leiden University Library (MS BPG 49a), *see* S. R. Melker, E. G. L. Schrijver and E. van Voolen (eds.), *The Image and Printed Book: Catalogue of an Exhibition Held at the Jewish Historical Museum,* Amsterdam 1990, pp.50–51, n° 17. According to the reproduction of the first page included in the catalogue (Fig. 22), it is obvious that the Hebrew in this manuscript too was not written by a Jewish hand.

49 Cf. M. Beit-Arié and C. Sirat, *Manuscrits médiévaux en caractères hébraïques portant des indications de date jusqu'à 1540,* II, Paris and Jerusalem 1979, n° 58. The Latin initial letters ER in fol. 5v, also reproduced in colours in Garel, *ibid.,* n° 21, p.35, represent the Hebrew initial word *erekh*. The letter R is vocalized in red ink by the Hebrew sign for the vowel *e*, while the missing last vocal *kh*, which could not have been accommodated by the space left for the initials, was written (and vocalized) in the right margin in the same ink and pen in Hebrew, but in reverse direction, to match the Latin left-to-right direction.

50 *See* L. Avrin, *Micrography as Art,* Paris and Jerusalem 1981.

51 *See,* for instance, Th. and M. Metzger, 'Les enluminures du Ms. Add. 11639 de la British Library: un manuscrit hébreu du Nord de la France (fin du XIIIe siècle - premier quart du XIVe siècle)', *Wiener Jahrbuch für Kunstgeschichte,* 38 (1985), pp.59–113, esp. 107–109.

52 Cf. B. Narkiss, 'An Illuminated Mishneh Torah Manuscript in the Jewish National and University Library in Jerusalem', *Kirjath Sepher,* 43 (1967–1968), pp.285–300 (in Hebrew). In this case the artist identified was Maestro di Ser Cambio of Perugia (*c.*1400).

53 *See* R. Suckale, 'Über den Anteil christlicher Maler an der Ausmalung hebräischer Handschriften der Gotik in Bayern', in M. Treml and J. Kirmeier (eds.), *Geschichte und Kultur der Juden in Bayern: Aufsätze,* München and New York 1988 (*Veröffentlichungen zur Bayerischen Geschichte und Kultur,* 17), p.130. The contours of the initial Hebrew word inscribed near the Latin inscription at the head of the Book of Job are written by a hand which was well trained in Hebrew writing, while the illustrated initial words in the manuscript are shaped in a rather crude and strange manner. Therefore it seems that the Latin instructions for the illustration and the contours of the Hebrew initial words on the margins were written by a Jew, probably the main scribe himself, whereas a non-Jewish artist (or artists), who illustrated the initial words, also depicted them in gold.

54 *See* in detail M. Beit-Arié, 'A Palaeographical and Codicological Study of the Manuscript' in *The Rothschild Miscellany: a Scholarly Commentary* [to a facsimile edition], Jerusalem and London 1989, pp.97–100.

55 *See* C. O. Nordström, *The Duke of Alba's Castilian Bible: a Study of the Rabbinical Features of the Miniatures,* Stockholm 1967; S. Fellous, 'Une Bible à la rencontre des cultures', in *Le Livre au Moyen Age,* [Paris] 1988, pp.148–154; idem, 'Catalogue Raisoné of the Miniatures', in the *Companion Volume* of the facsimile edition of the manuscript, *La Biblia de Alba: an Illustrated Manuscript Bible in Castilian* (ed. J. Schonfield) Madrid 1992, pp.78–146.

56 A. Keller, 'The Making of the Biblia de Alba', in the *Companion Volume* of the facsimile edition, p.152.

NOTES TO LECTURE II

1 *Sefarad* is a biblical geographical term (Ob. 1:20), interpreted in the Middle Ages as designating Spain.

2 *See* M. Beit-Arié, 'Hebrew Script in Spain: Development, Offshoots and Vicissitudes' (cf. above, Lecture I, note 5), pp.287–288 and Figs.19–24 (for a detailed presentation of the Sefardic scripts *see* the entire paper, pp.282–317). The Sefardic type of Hebrew scripts must have been introduced into Christian Spain by scribes and scholars who fled from Andalusia in the middle of the twelfth century and settled there (and also in Provence), following the Almohad invasion and the destruction of Jewish centres.

3 It seems that the Jews in the Orient did not manufacture their own parchment for codices, but were dependent on Arabic production, as is reflected by halakhic discussion concerning the adoption of the *raqq,* the Arabic parchment, for Jewish ritual scrolls. On the halakhic problem posed by Arabic parchment, its rejection and *post facto* acceptance by rabbinic authorities, *see* M. Haran, 'Bible Scrolls in Eastern and Western Jewish Communities from Qumran to the High Middle Ages', *HUCA,* 56 (1985), pp.47–56.

4 Cf. E. Ashtor, *Levant Trade in the Later Middle Ages,* Princeton 1983, p.210, note 63; idem. 'Levantine Sugar Industry in the Later Middle Ages: an Example of Technological Decline', *Israel Oriental Studies,* 7 (1977), pp.266–273. In later periods, Italian paper mills produced special papers destined for export to the Islamic Orient which contained particular watermark designs, consisting mainly of the Muslim symbol of the crescent. Cf. F. Babinger, 'Papierhandel und Papierbereitung in der Levante', *Wochenblatt für Papierfabrikation,* 62 (1931), pp.1215–1219 [= F. Babinger, *Aufsätze und Abhandlungen zur Geschichte Südosteuropas und der Levante,* II, Munich 1966 (*Südosteuropa-Schriften,* 8), pp.127–132]; V. Mošin and M. Grozdanović-Pajić, '"Crown Star Crescent" Mark and European Export Paper', *Papiergeschichte,* 13 (1963), pp.44–51.

5 *See Hebrew Codicology,* pp.27–36, and the studies referred to. For the characterization of Arabic papers according to Arabic sources published by J. Karabacek, *see* C.-M. Briquet, *Le papier arabe au Moyen-Age et sa fabrication,* Berne 1888 (an off-print from *Union de la Papeterie,* août-septembre) [= *Briquet's Opuscula,* Hilversum 1955 (*Monumenta Chartae Papyraceae Historiam Illustrantia,* 4), pp.162–170]. On two-layer, double-face paper, *see* J. Karabacek, 'Das arabische Papier', *Mittheilungen aus der Sammlung der Papyrus Erzherzog Rainer,* II-III, Vienna 1887, pp.140–141; cf. the recent English translation of most of Karabacek's study by D. Baker and S. Dittmer, *Arab Paper,* London 1991, p.53; J. Irigoin, 'La datation par les filigranes du papier', *Codicologia* (ed. A. Gruys), V (*Litterae textuales*), Leiden 1980, p.15; H. Gachet, 'Papier et parchemin', *IPH Information,* 16 (1982), pp.36–41; J. Pederson, *The Arabic Book* (tr. G. French), Princeton 1984, p.66.

6 No typology exists of the codicological practices of Arabic manuscripts. While my characterization of Hebrew codicological features is based on quantitative study of most of the dated manuscripts, for Arabic manuscripts I have had to rely only upon occasional examination of Arabic codices, a few catalogues which provide codicological data, and information received from my colleague, Ephraim Wust, keeper of Arabic manuscripts in the Jewish National and University Library of Jerusalem, and my remarks should be regarded as tentative. For the Hebrew Oriental manuscripts *see Hebrew Codicology,* pp.74–75, 78–83, 86. On the five bifolia quiring which also characterizes Arabic manuscripts *see* Fr. Déroche, *Catalogue des manuscrits arabes [de la] Bibliothèque nationale,* Deuxième partie, Tome I, 1: *Les manuscrits du Coran: aux origines de la calligraphie coranique,* Paris 1983, p.20, note 6; on the practice of four bifolia quiring in early Arabic Korans produced in Iran *see* idem, Tome I, 2: *Les manuscrits du Coran du Maghreb à l'Insulinde,* Paris 1985, p.14, and particularly the individual descriptions of the Persian manuscripts in Fr. Richard, *Catalogue des manuscrits persans [de la] Bibliothèque nationale,* I, Paris 1989. On *quinion* quiring of Syriac codices, *see* M. H. Goshen – Gottstein, *Syriac Manuscripts in the Harvard College Library,* Ann Arbor 1979 (*Harvard Semitic Studies,* 23), p.25, note 55.

7 *Hebrew Codicology,* pp.75–76. Access to the great collection of early Hebrew codices in the Russian National Library (formerly Saltykov–Shchedrin State Public Library) of St Petersburg, denied until recently, has enabled us to trace back the special Sefardic practice of pricking both outer and inner margins and ruling two (sometimes four) successive leaves of the folded quire at once (always on the hair side of the first page of each pair) to the end of the tenth century. While the earliest dated Spanish manuscript displaying this technique is dated 1184 (it is also the earliest dated Sefardic manuscript in Western collections), much earlier dated codices, produced by immigrant scribes from the Maghreb in Palestine, which are kept in St Petersburg, have recently been found to have been ruled in accordance with the peculiar Sefardic practice: MSS EBP. IIB39, written in Jerusalem in 988/9 and EBP. IIB8 written in 1050/1 in Palestine (by the scribe of MS Cairo, Karaite Synagogue written in 1027/8 [cf. *Hebrew Codicology,* p.111, addendum to p.15, note 10], which is similarly pricked and ruled). The variant Sefardic practice of pricking the outer margins only and ruling two successive unfolded bifolia can be noticed already in part of MS EBP. IIB124, produced in Kairouan (Tunisia) between 941 and 1030 (the date in the colophon is partly illegible).

8 Cf. A. Keller, 'Le système espagnol de réglure dans les manuscrits visigothiques', *VIII Coloquio del Comité internacional de paleografia latina: Actas* (Madrid-Toledo, 29 setiembre - 1 octubre 1987), Madrid 1989 (*Estudios y Ensayos,* 6), pp.107–114; idem, 'Codicologia comparativa de los manuscritos medievales españoles, latinos, arabes y hebreos', in *Estudios sobre Alfonso VI y la Reconquista de Toledo: Actas del II Congreso Internacional de Estudios Mozárabes* (Toledo, 20–26 mayo 1985), III, Toledo 1989 (*Serie Histórica,* 5), pp.207–218.

9 According to Rand, quoted by J. Vezin in *Annuaire de l'Ecole Pratique des Hautes Etudes,* IVème section, 109 (1976–1977), p.493, such a ruling characterized many Latin manuscripts produced in Spain before the twelfth century. *See also* J. Vezin, 'La réalisation matérielle des manuscrits latins pendant le haut Moyen Age', *Codicologica* (ed. A. Gruys), II (*Litterae textuales),* Leiden 1978, p.33.

10 *Ashkenaz* is a biblical geographical term (Gen. 10:3; I Chron. 1:6; Jer: 51:27) assigned to designate northern France and particularly Germany in the Middle Ages.

11 I have benefitted from a tentative diachronic survey by Albert Derolez, 'Quires and Ruling in Western Manuscripts from the Ninth to the Fifteenth Century', and from the drafts of a manual of Latin codicology which is being prepared by J. Peter Gumbert, both presented to the Comparative Codicology Group, which I was privileged to coordinate at the Institute for Advanced Studies of the Hebrew University in Jerusalem in the winter and spring of 1991.

12 The study of all the dated Ashkenazic manuscripts shows that at the end of the twelfth century a new processing technique emerged, minimizing the

natural difference between the hair-side and the flesh-side of the parchment and resulting in a complete or almost complete equalization of both sides in most of the Hebrew parchment manuscripts produced in Germany from the middle of the thirteenth century onwards. In manuscripts produced in northern France the parchment sides are still discernable, at least in part (cf. *Hebrew Codicology*, pp.22–26). The Ashkenazic typical 'new' parchment seems to correspond with the characterization of the parchment employed in Latin manuscripts produced in Europe. Cf. W. Wattenbach, *Das Schrift-wesen im Mittelalter*, Leipzig 1896, pp.116–117; L. Santifaller, *Beiträge zur Geschichte der Beschreibstoffe im Mittelalter*, I (*Mitteilungen des Instituts für österreichische Geschichtsforschungen*, XVI, 1), Graz and Cologne 1953, pp.80–82; M. Palma; 'Modifiche di alcuni aspetti materiali della produzione libraria latina nei secoli XII e XIII', *Scrittura e Civiltà*, 12 (1988), p.123. On a halakhic source testifying that at the end of the Middle Ages it was impossible to distinguish the parchment sides in *Ashkenaz, see* M. Glatzer, 'The Aleppo Codex' (cf. above, Lecture I, note 32), p.190.

13 To this day it is not clear whether the 'new' practice of pricking both outer and inner margins for guiding the horizontal ruling, introduced into Ashkenazic continental manuscripts in the early thirteenth century and characterizing most of the Ashkenazic codices from the late thirteenth century on (cf. *Hebrew Codicology*, pp.70–71), is also typical of Latin Franco-German manuscripts of the late Middle Ages, as it is of insular ones. *See* Beit-Arié, *The Only Dated* etc., pp.26–27, note 65. *See also* J. Vezin in *Annuaire* (cf. above, note 9), p.495.

14 Cf. C. T. Schonemann, *Versuch eines vollständigen Systems der allgemeinen besonders älteren Diplomatik*, I, Leipzig 1818, p.515; E. A. Loew, *The Beneventan Script*, Oxford 1914, pp.293–294; N. R. Ker, *English Manuscripts in the Century after the Norman Conquest*, Oxford 1960, pp.41–42; J. Vezin, 'Les manuscrits datés de l'ancien fonds latin de la Bibliothèque nationale de Paris', *Scriptorium*, 19 (1965), p.87; idem, *Annuaire*, p.494; idem, *Codicologica*, II, pp.33–34. On the spread of colour ruling in Latin Gothic manuscripts produced all over Occidental Europe, including Italy (where Hebrew manuscripts were rarely ruled by plummet) *see* the survey of ninety-five dated and localized manuscripts carried out by M. Palma, *ibid.* (cf. above, note 12), pp.119–133.

15 Cf. *Hebrew Codicology*, pp.76–78, 84. The earliest Hebrew manuscript ruled entirely by plummet seems to be MS Oxford, Corpus Christi College 133, which must have been in England (or produced there) before 1200 (cf. above, p.8).

16 *Ibid.*, p.73, note 139.

17 Cf. J. Vezin in *Codicologica*, II, p.34.

18 *Hebrew Codicology*, pp.78 and 113.

19 A. Derolex, *Codicologie des manuscrits en écriture humanistique sur parchemin*, I–II, Turnhout 1984.

20 *Hebrew Codicology*, p.110. Cf. also Beit-Arié, 'The Codicological Data-Base' etc. (cf. above, Lecture I, note 16), pp.191–194 (Appendixes VIIa–VIId).

21 'The Shop of a Florentine "cartolario" in 1426', *Studi offerti a Roberto Ridolfi* (*Biblioteca di Bibliografia Italiana*, 71), Florence 1973, pp.237–248, esp. pp.240, 244–245 (nos. 48–50). For additional references *see* Derolez, *ibid.*, I, pp.35 (note 11) and 78.

22 *Ibid.*, pp.77–78.

23 J. P. Gumbert, 'Ruling by Rake and Board', in P. Ganz (ed.), *The Role of the Book in Medieval Culture: Proceedings of the Oxford International Symposium . . . 1982*, Turnhout 1986 (*Bibliologia*, 3), pp.44–48.

24 J. Irigoin, 'Pour une étude des centres de copie byzantins', *Scriptorium*, 12 (1958), pp.208–227; J. Leroy, 'Les manuscrits grecs d'Italie', *Codicologica*, II, pp.52–66.

25 I am indebted to Prof. Axinia Džurova for drawing my attention to this similarity. For Greek decorations, compare, for instance, I. Hutter, *Corpus der byzantinischen Miniaturenhandschriften*, I, Stuttgart 1977 (*Denkmäler der Buchkunst*, 2), nos. 39 (pls. 227–235), 44 (pl. 285), 48 (pl. 298–299), 62 (pls. 388–391). For Slavonic decorations *see* A. Džurova, *Bulgarian Manuscripts: a Thousand Years of Ornaments and Miniatures*, Sofia 1981 (in Bulgarian); A. Džurova, K. Stančev and M. Japundžić, *Catalogo dei manuscritti slavi della Biblioteca Vaticana*, Sofia 1985. *See also* Ch. Paschou, 'Style "Balkanique" dans la décoration de quelques manuscrits de la Bibliothèque nationale d'Athènes', *Paléographie et diplomatique slaves*, vol. 2, Sofia 1985, pp.214–225.

26 Cf. E. J. Worman, 'Two Book-Lists from the Cambridge Genizah Fragments', *JQR*, 20 (1908), p.459, line 16.

27 Cf., for example, J.-P. Rothschild, 'Listes des livres hébreux en Italie: nouveaux documents pour une typologie', *RHT*, 19 (1989), pp.304, line 11 and 318, line 4 ('Ashkenazic writing', i.e. German) and pp.303, line 2; 304, line 12; 305, line 59; 327, line 1 ('French writing').

28 Worman, *ibid.*, line 27.

29 E.g., Rothschild, *ibid.*, pp.304, line 8 and 305, line 58.

30 E.g., J.-P. Rothschild . 'Quelques listes de livres hébreux dans des manuscrits de la Bibliothèque nationale de Paris', *RHT*, 17 (1987), p.319, lines 4 and 7. The term appears also in various halakhic sources.

31 *See*, for instance, W. Wright, *Catalogue of the Syriac Manuscripts in the British Museum*, III, London 1872, pls. II, VII, X, XIV, XVIII and XIX, and particularly the plates in P. Kokowzoff, *Nouveaux fragments syropalestiniens de la Bibliothèque impériale publique de Saint-Pétersbourg*, St Petersburg 1906.

32 Cf. Déroche, *Catalogue* (above, note 6), I, 1, pl. VII.

33 Cf. B. Moritz, *Arabic Palaeography*, Cairo 1905 (reprinted Osnabrück 1986), most of plates 1–45; G. Vajda, *Album de paléographie arabe*, Paris 1958, nos. 1–6; A. J. Arberry, *The Koran Illuminated: a Handlist of the Korans in the Chester Beatty Library*, Dublin 1967, pls. 1, 11, 12 and 17; M. Lings and Y. H. Safadi, *The Qur'an: Catalogue of an Exhibition of Qur'an Manuscripts at*

the British Library, London 1976, pp.17–28; D. James, *Qur'ans and Bindings from the Chester Beatty Library: a Facsimile Exhibition,* London 1980, pp.13–24. *See also* the illuminating historical analysis of the ductus, particularly the direction of the executed strokes, in the Hebrew scripts in comparison to other Semitic scripts and Greek, by Colette Sirat in collaboration with Michèle Dukan, *Ecriture et civilisations,* Paris 1976, pp.4–17, 95–101. Sirat concludes that the ductus of Hebrew scripts changed in accordance with the ductus of the dominating non-Hebrew scripts. On the Kufic ductus and its impact on the Oriental Hebrew script *see* pp.99–101.

34 Cf. the plates in M. Ocaña Jiménez, *El cúfico hispano y su evolución,* Madrid 1970.

35 Cf. R. Barbour, *Greek Literary Hand A. D. 400–1600,* Oxford 1981, plates 1–3 and G. Cavallo, *Ricerche sulla maiuscola biblica,* Florence 1967 (*Studi e testi di papirologia editi dall'Istituto papirologico 'G. Vitelli' di Firenze,* 2); B. M. Metzger, *Manuscripts of the Greek Bible: an Introduction to Greek Paleography,* New York and Oxford 1981, pp. 24–25. Compare also the 'square' style of the Coptic script in W. H. Worrell, *The Coptic Manuscripts in the Freer Collection,* New York 1923.

36 Cf. M. P. Brown, *A Guide to Western Historical Scripts from Antiquity to 1600,* London 1990, no.1.

37 Cf. N. Abbott, *The Rise of the North Arabic Script and its Ḳur'ānic Development, with a Full Description of the Ḳur'ān Manuscripts in the Oriental Institute,* Chicago 1939, pp.23–28.

38 Cf. Lings and Safadi, *The Qur'an,* pp.42–47; M. Lings, *The Quranic Art of Calligraphy and Illumination,* England 1976, pp.53–69.

39 M. P. Brown, *Guide,* p.2.

40 The term 'Rabbinic' was already rejected by Solomon A. Birnbaum, who laid the foundation of modern Hebrew palaeography as far as the typology and history of scripts are concerned, in his pioneering *The Hebrew Scripts,* vol. I, Leiden 1971; vol. II, London 1954–1957. Birnbaum replaced 'Rabbinic' by '*Mashait*' (cf. I, cols. 189–190), a late medieval Ashkenazic corrupted form of *al-Mashq,* an Arabic calligraphic term employed in Sefardic sources to designate the semi-cursive mode of script; cf. M. Beit-Arié (in collaboration with E. Angel and A. Yardeni), *Specimens of Mediaeval Hebrew Scripts,* I, Jerusalem 1987, pp.10–12. *See also,* A. Gacek, 'Early Qur'anic Fragments', *Fontanus,* 3 (1990), p.46, on a description of the *al-Mashq* script in a ninth-century Arabic work.

41 Joseph Ibn Migash (1077–1141), cited by Maimonides in one of his responsa, written in Arabic; cf. Beit-Arié, *ibid.,* p.11.

42 M. G. I. Lieftinck, 'Pour une nomenclature de l'écriture livresque de la période dite gothique', *Nomenclature des écritures livresques du IXe au XVIe siècle: Premier colloque international de paléographie latine, Paris 28–30 avril 1953* (*Colloques internationaux du Centre National de la Recherche Scientifique, Sciences humaines,* 4), Paris 1954, pp.15–34.

43 Cf. M. P. Brown, loc. cit. It should be noted that the medieval Hebrew translation of Maimonides' responsum which cites the threefold classification by Ibn Migash, employs the term *beinoni* (medium) to designate the semi-cursive grade (cf. Beit-Arié, loc. cit.). Thus we are indeed using the Hebrew equivalent of the term *media* in our Hebrew nomenclature.

44 Cf. A. Yardeni, *The Book of Hebrew Script*, Jerusalem 1991 (in Hebrew), p.222.

45 For methodological aspects of script analysis in general and the characterization of the Hebrew script in particular, *see* C. Sirat, *L'examen des écritures: l'œil et la machine; essai de méthodologie*, Paris 1981. For practical quantitative methods of analyzing Hebrew script *see* A. Yardeni, *Hebrew Script*, and E. Engel, *The Development of the Hebrew Script from the Period of the Bar-Kokhba Revolt to 1000 A.D.* (Ph.D. thesis), Jerusalem 1990 (in Hebrew).

46 Cf. Yardeni, *Hebrew Script*, pp.76–77 and 188.

47 Sirat, *L'examen*, pp.35–44.

48 *See* Déroche, I/1, p.65, no. 12 (BN MS Arab.330f) and pl. VIII (mistakenly referring to no. 11, as is obvious from the indication of the folio and the number of lines). Déroche reconstructs the original size of the trimmed folio as 370×280mm. The dimension of the written space is 305×220mm.

49 Lings and Safadi, *The Qur'an*, p.17; Déroche, I/1, p.19. Déroche realized that the width of the written space is larger by 70mm than the written height in most of the Kufic fragments in his catalogue, while in the smallest formats it is larger by 50mm. *See also* the illuminating grid of the dimensions of the written space of all the manuscripts in pl.XXIV.

50 Déroche, I/1, pp.19 and 50. Hebrew fragments of oblong quires of various non-biblical texts, resembling the small format Kufic Korans, can be found in the Cairo Genizah, and seem to date before the eleventh century. Oblong small format codices, particularly containing liturgical texts, were sometimes produced in later periods in North Africa, where this format continued to be used occasionally by Arabic scribes until the fourteenth century after it had been abandoned in the East in the eleventh (cf. M. Lings, *The Quranic Art of Calligraphy and Illumination*, p.18). Small format calligraphic manuscripts, containing only one pericope of the Pentateuch, like the Kufic Kuranic manuscripts containing a single *sura*, were produced in Persia from the eleventh to the thirteenth century, bearing witness in their size, layout and decoration to the strong influence of Arabic calligraphy; cf. Beit-Arié and Sirat, *Manuscrits médiévaux* (above, Lecture I, note 49), II, no. 2. Similar as they are to the early Kufic Korans, even these manuscripts are not oblong in format and layout.

51 Exceptions among the early Greek codices are two fourth-century manuscripts: Codex Sinaiticus of exceptionally large format resembling the early Hebrew Bibles, and written in four columns, and Codex Vaticanus, which has three columns; cf. E. G. Turner, *The Typology of the Early Codex*, [Philadelphia] 1977, Table 16, p.134. It is worth mentioning that as in the

four-column Codex Sinaiticus (cf. Metzger [above, note 35], p.76 and plates 25–26 of the two opening layouts in *Mise en page et mise en texte du livre manuscrit*, [Paris] 1990, pp.62–65.), the Books of Psalms, Proverbs and Job were written in two columns in Hebrew three-column biblical manuscripts. The exceptional disposition of these books in Codex Sinaiticus may reflect the influence of the Jewish practice and corroborate H. J. M. Milne and T. C. Skeat's conclusion that it was most probably produced in Caesarea (Palestine); cf. Ph. Mayerson, 'Codex Sinaiticus: An Historical Observation', *Biblical Archaeologist*, Winter 1983, pp.54–56.

52 *See* Moritz, *Arabic Palaeography*, plates 119 (dated 923), 117, 127, 128, etc.; Vajda, *Album*, plates 11, 35, 72 (where the device is used at the end of almost every line, as in some Yemenite Hebrew manuscripts) and 177.

53 Lings and Safadi, *The Qur'an*, no. 85.

54 Abbott, *The Rise*, p.41.

55 Lings and Safadi, *The Qur'an*, no. 49. For the roundness of the Maghribī script, particularly in the late Middle Ages, *see* Moritz, *Arabic Palaeography*, plates 175–188, and Vajda, *Album*, plate 48. On the wavy and elliptical strokes of the Maghribī script *see* O. V. Houdas, 'Essai sur l'écriture maghrebine', *Nouveaux Mélanges Orientaux*, Paris 1886, p.106.

56 Lings and Safadi, *The Qur'an*, no. 54.

57 Lings and Safadi, *The Qur'an*, no. 151.

58 M. P. Brown, *Guide*, no. 25. The nomenclature of the Latin scripts used henceforth follows Brown's terminology. Cf. also the German specimens of the transitional script between late Caroline and early Gothic in K. Schneider, *Gotische Schriften in deutscher Sprache*, I, Wiesbaden 1987, plates 1–29.

59 M. P. Brown, *Guide*, no. 32; cf. also plate 29 of the *textualis quadrata* script. *See also* the confrontation of Latin and Hebrew Gothic scripts in Sirat, *L'examen des écritures*, illustrations XIII–XV and the discussion on p.39.

60 Compare plate 30 to Brown, *Guide*, plate 39.

61 Cf. Brown, *Guide*, pp.116–117.

62 *See* M. Beit-Arié, 'The Cryptic Name of the Scribe Abraham b. Yom Tov ha-Cohen', *Israel Oriental Studies*, 2(1972), pp.51–56 (*see also Kiryat Sefer*, 56, 1980–1981, pp.546–547).

63 MS Cambridge (Mass.), Harvard College Library, Houghton Library Riant 20, fol. 69r, a Gospel Book written in Italy in the first half of the twelfth century in a smaller format. Cf. L. Light, *The Bible in the Twelfth Century: An Exhibition of Manuscripts at the Houghton Library*, Cambridge (Mass.) 1988, no.5.

64 MS Cambridge (Mass.), Houghton Library Typ 489, fol. 78r, Pope Bonifacius VIII, *Liber sextus Decretalium* with a commentary, a *pecia* copy produced in Bologna in the late fourteenth century; cf. W. H. Bond, *Supplement to the Census of Medieval and Renaissance Manuscripts in the United States and Canada*, New York 1962, p.281; *Marks in Books, Illustrated and Explained*, Cambridge

(Mass.), Houghton Library, 1985 no. 31. Compare also Brown, *Guide*, plate 48.

65 A. G. Watson, *Catalogue of Dated and Datable Manuscripts c.700–1600 in the Department of Manuscripts, The British Library*, London 1979, vol. I, p.280, no. 64; vol. II, plate 368. Compare also MS British Library Eg. 818, Fig.28 in B. L. Ullman, *The Origin and Development of Humanistic Script*, Rome 1960, a twelfth-century manuscript which may have inspired Poggio Bracciolini's handwriting (*ibid.*, p.54), and Bracciolini's own book script in A. C. de la Mare, *The Handwriting of Italian Humanists*, Oxford 1973, plates XV–XVI. An example of a humanist manuscript which is perhaps more appropriate as a comparison to the Hebrew example is MS Vatican lat. 559, reproduced in A. Derolez, *Codicologie des manuscrits en écriture humanistique*, I, Fig.53.

66 Compare various plates in de la Mare, *Handwriting*.

67 A. Turyn, *Dated Greek Manuscripts of the Thirteenth and Fourteenth Centuries in the Libraries of Great Britain*, Washington DC 1980, pl. 88.

68 Compare also plate 64–70 in N. Wilson, *Medieval Greek Bookhands*, Plates, Cambridge (Mass.) 1972.

NOTES TO CHAPTER III

1 D. F. McKenzie, *Bibliography and the Sociology of Texts*, London 1986, p.13.

2 The common assumption of reading aloud in the Middle Ages has recently been challenged by P. Saenger, who argues that the separation of words in Latin manuscripts enabled and was later followed by silent reading and copying, well suited to monastic conditions. Cf. 'Manières de lire médiévales', in *Histoire de l'édition française*, I, Paris 1982, pp.131–141; 'Silent Reading: Its Impact on Late Medieval Script and Society', *Viator*, 13 (1983), pp.367–414. However, reading aloud while copying was practised among Hebrew scribes in late twelfth-century Germany, as is attested by *Sefer Hasidim*, the main source for our knowledge of Jewish scribal practices in medieval Europe; cf. *Das Buch der Frommen* (ed. J. Wistinezki), Berlin 1891, p.187, par. 733.

3 *See* L. Havet, *Manuel de critique verbal appliquée aux textes latins*, Paris 1911, pp.44–46.

4 Cf. the concise discussion of Byzantine literacy by R. Browning and of Western European literacy by P. Saenger in *Dictionary of the Middle Ages*, VII, New York 1986, pp.594–597, 597–602. *See also The Use of Literacy in Early Mediaeval Europe* (ed. R. McKitterick), Cambridge 1990, particularly S. Kelly's contribution, 'Anglo-Saxon Lay Societies and the Written Word', pp.36–81, and 'Conclusion' by R. McKitterick, pp.328–331, regarding evidence of literacy among certain sections of secular society, especially the administrative classes.

Cf. recently B. Bedos-Rezak, 'The Confrontation of Orality and Textuality: Jewish and Christian Literacy in Eleventh- and Twelfth-Century Northern France', *Rashi 1040–1990: Congrès européen des Études juives* (ed. G. Sed-Rajna), Paris 1993, pp. 541–558.

5 *See* M. Güdemann, *Geschichte des Erziehungswesens und der Cultur der Juden in Frankreich und Deutschland*, I–III, Vienna 1880–1888; N. Morris, *A History of Jewish Education*, I–III, Jerusalem 1960–1977 (in Hebrew); S. D. Goitein, *A Mediterranean Society*, II, Berkeley, Los Angeles and London, 1971, pp.173–190 (on women teachers and the education of girls: pp.183–185).

6 *See* B. Smalley, *The Study of the Bible in the Middle Ages*, p.78.

7 *See* B. Dodge, *Muslim Education in Medieval Times*, Washington, D.C. 1962, pp.3–5.

8 *See* the concise outlines of the history of Latin book production by R. H. Rouse in *Dictionary of the Middle Ages*, VIII, New York 1987, pp.100–105. On the early beginnings of commercial lay production in Paris *see*, recently, Richard H. and Mary A. Rouse, 'The Commercial Production of Manuscript Books in Late-Thirteenth-Century and Early-Fourteenth-Century Paris', *Medieval Book Production: Assessing the Evidence* (ed. L. L. Brownrigg), Anderson-Lovelace 1990 (*Proceedings of the Second Conference of the Seminar in the History of the Book to 1500, Oxford, July 1988*), pp.103–115.

9 Cf. R. S. Mackensen, 'Moslem Libraries and Sectarian Propaganda', *The American Journal of Semitic Languages and Literatures*, 51 (1934–1935), p.108; Y. Eche, *Les bibliothèques arabes publiques et semi-publiques en Mésopotamie, en Syrie et en Égypte au Moyen Age*, Damascus 1967, p.273–275.

10 Eche, *ibid.*, pp.23–24, 85–87, 113, 380.

11 *See* Eche's book, and R. S. Mackensen's series of articles, *AJSLL*, 51 (1934–1935), pp.83–113; 114–125; 52 (1935–1936), pp.22–23, 104–110; 245–253; 53 (1936–1937), pp.239–250; 54 (1937), pp.41–61; 56 (1939), pp.149–157. *See also* the survey by M. Lesley Wilkins, 'Islamic Libraries' in the forthcoming *Encyclopedia of Library History* (eds. W. Weigand and D. Davis) to be published by Garland Press. (I am indebted to Mrs. Wilkins for kindly enabling me to use the typescript of her entry.)

12 Cf. above, Lecture I, note 16, and the paper referred to, pp.167–168.

13 Such as MS Rome, Biblioteca Casanatense 3104, produced in Spain in the fifteenth century, in which the scribe states in the colophon that he copied the kabbalistic compilation 'for whoever may wish to purchase it.' Other impersonal copies may be traced by colophons which refer to unnamed owners, or which leave a blank space for inserting the owner's name (as in the colophon of MS. Holon, Y. Nahum's private collection 302.1, written in San'a in 1434). A few manuscripts written as undestined copies were later sold by their copyists, who inscribed the deeds of sale, such as MS Parma, Biblioteca Palatina 2157, sold in Italy in 1428.

14 Cf. Beit-Arié, 'The Codicological Data-Base' (above, Lecture I, note 16), p.178, note 5.

15 Cf. M. Beit-Arié, 'Palaeographical Identification of Hebrew Manuscripts: Methodology and Practice', *Jewish Art*, 12 (1986/87), p.18.

16 *Ibid.* p.16.

17 A. Petrucci, 'Il libro manoscritto', in *Letteratura italiana*, vol. II: *Produzione e consumo*, Turin 1983, pp.512–513, 520–522, referred to by R. Chartier, *L'ordre des livres*, Aix-en-Provence 1992, pp.63–64.

18 Cf. R. Mackensen, 'Arabic Books and Libraries in the Umayyad Period', *The American Journal of Semitic Languages and Literatures*, 52 (1935–1936), p.250. On books copied by Arabic scholars *see* Eche, *Les bibliothèques arabes*, pp.284–285.

19 *See* M. M. Sibai, *Mosque Libraries: an Historical Study*, London and New York 1987, p.41; Fr. Rosenthal, *The Technique and Approach of Muslim Scholarship*, Rome 1947 (*Analecta Orientalia*, 24), pp.9–10.

20 On the controlled process of producing books in the Frankenthal scriptorium, *see* the illuminating analysis by A. Cohen-Mushlin, *A Medieval Scriptorium: Sancta Maria Magdalena de Frankendal*, I–II, Wiesbaden 1990 (*Wolfenbüteler Mittelalter-Studies*, 3). Cf. also M.-C. Garand, 'Manuscrits monastiques et scriptoria aux XIᵉ et XIIᵉ siècles', *Codicologica*, III, Leiden 1980, pp.9–33.

21 *See* in detail M. Beit-Arié, 'Transmission of Texts by Scribes and Copyists: Unconscious and Critical Interferences', *Bulletin of the John Rylands University Library of Manchester*, 75, no. 3 (Autumn/Winter 1993) [=Proceedings of *Artifacts and Texts: The Re-Creation of Classical Jewish Literature in Medieval Hebrew Manuscripts*, a Conference held at the John Rylands Research Institute, 28–30 April 1992] (forthcoming).

22 Cf. also I. Ta-Shma, 'The "Open" Book in Medieval Hebrew Literature – The Problem of Authorized "Editions"', *Proceedings* (*see* note 21).

23 *See* S. Morison, *Politics and Script: Aspects of Authority and Freedom in the Development of Graeco-Latin Script from the Sixth Century B.C. to the Twentieth Century A.D.* (ed. N. Barker), Oxford 1972 (*The Lyell Lectures 1957*).

24 On the expressive function of typography, *see* McKenzie, *Bibliography and the Sociology of Texts*, esp. pp.2, 8–9, 12–13, 24, 47, and the referred studies.

25 Cf. C. Bozzolo, D. Coq, D. Muzerelle, E. Ornato, 'Noir et blanc: Premiers résultats d'une enquête sur la mise en page dans le livre médiéval', *Il libro e il testo: Atti del convegno internazionale, Urbino, 20–23 settembre 1982* (ed. C. Questa and R. Raffaelli), Urbino 1984, pp.197–221; R. Bergeron and E. Ornato, 'La lisibilité dans les manuscrits et les imprimés de la fin du Moyen-Age: Préliminaires d'une recherche', *Scrittura e Civiltà*, 14 (1990), pp.151–198.

26 On proportions of page format and written space and the harmony between

size and layout, particularly in printed books, *see* J. Tschichold, 'Non-Arbitrary Proportions of Page and Type Area', *Calligraphy and Palaeography: Essays Presented to Alfred Fairbank on his 70th Birthday*, London 1965, pp.179–191. On proportions of manuscripts *see* L. Gilissen, *Prolégomènes à la codicologie*, Ghent 1977, pp.125–249.

27 M. B. Parkes, 'The Influence of the Concepts of *ordinatio* and *compilatio* on the Development of the Book', *Medieval Learning and Literature: Essays Presented to Richard William Hunt* (ed. J. J. G. Alexander and M. T. Gibson), Oxford 1976, pp.115–141 [=M. B. Parkes, *Scribes, Scripts and Readers: Studies in the Communication and Dissemination of Medieval Texts*, London and Riò Grande 1991, pp.35–70]; R. H. and M. A. Rouse, '*Statim invenire*: Schools, Preachers and New Attitude to the Page', *Renaissance and Renewal in the Twelfth Century* (ed. R. L. Benson and G. Constable), Oxford 1982, pp.201–225. *See also* the papers in the section 'Glossed Books as an Instrument of Continuity and Change' in *The Role of the Book in Medieval Culture: Proceedings of the Oxford International Symposium, 26 September – 1 October 1982* (ed. P. Ganz), II, Turnhout 1986 (*Bibliologia*, 4), pp.75–128.

28 Cf. M. Beit-Arié, 'Hebrew Manuscript Collections in Leningrad and their Importance to the History of the Hebrew Book', *Jewish Studies*, 31 (1991), pp.33–46 (in Hebrew).

29 Cf. Glatzer, 'The Aleppo Codex' (above, Lecture I, note 32).

30 *See* the many illustrations in L. Avrin, *Micrography as Art*, Paris and Jerusalem 1981.

31 Cf. M. Camille, 'The Book of Signs: Writing and Visual Difference in Gothic Manuscript Illumination', *Word & Image*, 1 (1985), p.138.

32 Cr. J. Irigoin, 'Livre et texte dans les manuscrits byzantins de poètes', *Il libro e il testo: Atti del convegno internazionale, Urbino 20–23 settembre 1982* (ed. C. Questa and R. Raffaelli), Urbino 1984, pp.87–102; N. G. Wilson, 'The Relation of Text and Commentary in Greek Books', *ibid.*, pp.105–110.

33 Cf. L. Holtz, 'Les manuscrits latins à gloses et à commentaires de l'antiquité à l'époque carolingienne', *ibid.* pp.141–167. *See also* various chapters and plates in *Mise en page et mise en texte du livre manuscrit* (sous la direction de H.-J. Martin and J. Vezin), [Paris] 1990. Koranic commentaries in Arabic manuscripts were always interwoven with the Koranic text, and only supercommentaries were copied in the margins; cf. A. F. Beetson in *Arabic Literature to the End of the Umayyad Period* (eds. A. F. Beetson et al), Cambridge 1983, p.24. Oriental Judeo-Arabic biblical commentaries by Karaite scholars were similarly presented. On the Persian practice of multi-layered manuscripts, which displayed two parallel disparate texts of the same genre, cf. *ibid.*, p.25.

34 *See* C. F. R. De Hamel, *Glossed Books of the Bible and the Origins of the Paris Booktrade*, Woodbridge and Dover (NH) 1984, pp.14–22.

35 *Ibid.*, pp.21–27.

36 Prof. Menahem Schmelzer made this observation in his paper 'Some

Medieval Hebrew Prayer Books: Texts, Rubrics and Marginalia' at the conference *Artefact and Text* held at the John Rylands Research Institute in Manchester, 28–30 April 1992.

37 *See* the previous note. Cf. also *Illuminated Hebrew Manuscripts from the Library of the Jewish Theological Seminary of America*, New York 1965, no.13.

38 J. Mallon, *Paléographie romaine*, Madrid 1952 (*Scripturae: Monumenta et Studia, 3*), pp.22–23.

39 Cf. J. Gilissen, *L'expertise des écritures médiévales*, Ghent 1973, pp.20–32.

40 O. Valls i Subirà, *Paper and Watermarks in Catalonia*, I, Amsterdam 1970, p.6.

41 Idem, *The History of Paper in Spain*, I, Madrid 1978, pp.85ff, esp. pp.87 and 98. Cf. also E. Levi-Provençal, *Histoire de l'Espagne musulmane*, III, Paris 1950, pp.33–34.

42 P. Sj. van Koningsveld, *The Latin-Arabic Glossary of the Leiden University*, Leiden 1976, pp.23, 68 and note 80. J. Irigoin follows A. Blum's dating of the beginning of papermaking in Muslim Spain in the twelfth century; cf. 'Les premiers manuscrits grecs écrits sur papier et le problème du bombycin', *Scriptorium*, 4 (1950), p.200 [=*Griechische Kodikologie und Textüberlieferung* (ed. D. Halfinger), Darmstadt 1980, p.139]. A. Grohmann, *Arabische Paläographie*, I, Vienna 1967 (*Österreichische Akademie der Wissenschaften, Philosophisch-historische Klasse Denkschriften, 94/1*), p.101, refers to the earliest evidence, recorded by al-Idrīsī in 1154, of the high quality paper manufactured in Xativa, following J. Karabacek, 'Das arabischer Papier' (p. 39 in the English translation; cf. above, Lecture II, note 5).

43 Mosseri Collection, formerly L24, IV. 18 according to the microfilmed copy in the Institute of Microfilmed Hebrew Manuscripts at the Jewish National and University Library in Jerusalem, lines 15–17 (Cf. S. D. Goitein, *A Mediterranean Society*, I, Berkeley, Los Angeles and London 1967, pp.81 and 410, note 2).

44 Cf. M. Gil, *Palestine During the First Muslim Period (634–1099)*, II, Tel Aviv, 1983, p.688, no. 371, lines 3–5 (in Hebrew). On both documents, *see* in detail, M. Beit-Arié, 'The Contribution of the Fustat Geniza to Hebrew Palaeography', *Pe'amim*, 41 (Autumn 1989), p.38 (in Hebrew). The good quality of the paper produced in Tripoli was indeed attested by a contemporary Persian traveller; *see* Karabacek, *Arab Paper* (above, Lecture II, note 5), p.37. Cf. also *ibid.*, p.31.

45 In accordance with al-Idrīsī's later statement (cf. above, note 42).

46 Joseph ben Mose, *Leket Joscher*, (ed. J. Freimann), I, Berlin 1903, p.32. Cf. M. Beit-Arié, 'Palaeographical Identification', *Jewish Art*, 12–13 (1988/87), p.41, note 38.

47 Cf. Y. A. Dinari, *The Rabbis of Germany and Austria at the Close of the Middle Ages*, Jerusalem 1984, p.140 (in Hebrew).

48 Cf. N. Golb in N. Golb and O. Pritsak, *Khazarian Hebrew Documents of the Tenth Century*, Ithaca and London 1982, pp.83–84.

49 Both letters were published by J. Mann, *Texts and Studies in Jewish History*

and Literature, I, Cincinnati 1931, pp.21–23, and are discussed on pp.5–6, 10–12. See also Golb, *Khazarian,* pp.83–86.

50 On Ḥasdai Ibn Shaprut *see* E. Ashtor, *The Jews of Moslem Spain,* I, Philadelphia 1973, pp.155–227. On his diplomatic activities *see ibid.,* pp.164–181. Cf. also Mann, *Texts and Studies,* p.5, note 5.

51 *See* especially E. Fleischer, 'On the Emergence of Hebrew Secular Poetry in Spain', *Culture and Society in Medieval Jewry: Studies Dedicated to the Memory of Haim Hillel Ben-Sasson* (ed. M. Ben-Sasson et al), Jerusalem 1989, pp.207–209 (in Hebrew).

52 Ashtor, *The Jews,* I, pp.188–190 regards both epistles as private letters written by Ḥasdai on behalf of the Jews under Byzantine rule, assuming that he was granted permission from the caliph to approach the Byzantine court, and that they were composed in Hebrew, in order to stress the fact that they came from the Jewish courtier, since it was then customary in international relations to word diplomatic correspondence in the writer's own language.

53 Ashtor, *ibid.,* p.189, does not regard this as an acknowledgement, but remarks that 'Hasdai informs the emperor in an obiter dictum that the missive he had sent to the caliph had given him much joy.'

54 Included in the additional fragment which was discerned by Golb as deriving from the same folio; cf. Golb, *Khazarian,* p.84, line 5. In another legible line of this fragment there is a reference to 'your two sons' (*ibid.,* p.85). Golb, p.85, argues that this reference may imply that the letter was not addressed to Constantine VII, who had only one son, but rather to Romanus Lecapenus, his father-in-law, who ruled in 919–944, and had four legitimate sons, one of whom died in 931, while a second was appointed patriarch in 933.

55 *See* the fragmentary text of lines 20–21 in Mann, I, p.23.

56 The envoys brought manuscripts as gifts, one of which was an illuminated copy of Dioscorides' *Materia Medica* in the original Greek. After the arrival of a Greek monk sent by the emperor upon the caliph's request, Ḥasdai translated into Arabic a substantial number of plant names which had remained untranslated in the ninth century Arabic translation made in Baghdad (*see* Ashtor, pp.167–168). On the extensive Arabic chronicles of the Byzantine mission of 949 and the confusion with regard to the exact date, *see* Ashtor, pp.420–421, note 17. For translations of the two major Arabic sources, Ibn 'Idhārī and Ibn Ḥayyān as quoted by al-Makkarī, *see* respectively, *Histoire de l'Afrique et de l'Espagne intitulée al-Bayano'l-Mogrib* (translated and annotated by E. Fagnan), II, Algiers 1904, pp.353, 357 and *The History of the Mohammedan Dynasties in Spain: Extracted from the Nafḥu-t-Ṭíb min Ghosni-l-Andalusi-r-Rattíb wa Tarikh Lisánu-d-Dín Ibni-l-Khattíb by Ahmed ibn Mohammed al-Makkarí* (translated and annotated by Pascual de Gayangos), II, London 1843, pp.137–138, 140–142.